STUDIES IN ENGLISH LITERATURE

Volume XCIX

D.H. LAWRENCE
AND THE
PSYCHOLOGY OF RHYTHM

THE MEANING OF FORM IN
THE RAINBOW

by

PETER BALBERT

1974
MOUTON
THE HAGUE · PARIS

LIBRARY OF CONGRESS CATALOG CARD NUMBER: 74-84240

Printed in The Netherlands by Mouton & Co., The Hague

To Lynne,
who lives the metaphor

Brood on that country who expresses our will. She is America, once a beauty of magnificence, unparalleled, now a beauty with a leprous skin. She is heavy with child – no one knows if legitimate – and languishes in a dungeon whose walls are never seen. Now the first contractions of her fearsome labor begin – it will go on: no doctor exists to tell the hour. It is only known that false labor is not likely on her now, no, she will probably give birth, and to what? . . .

from *The Armies of the Night*
by Norman Mailer

TABLE OF CONTENTS

1. CONCEPTION

A. THE PSYCHOLOGY OF RHYTHM

In a characteristically facetious discussion of his psychoanalytic essays, D. H. Lawrence wrote:

One last weary little word. This pseudo-philosophy of mine — "pollyanalytics," as one of my respected critics might say — is deduced from the novels and poems, not the reverse. The novels and poems come unwatched out of one's pen. And then the absolute need which one has for some sort of satisfactory attitude toward oneself and things in general makes one try to abstract some definite conclusions from one's experience as a writer and as a man. The novels and the poems are pure passionate experience. These 'pollyanalytics' are inferences made afterwards from the experience.[1]

It would be unwise to accept, without qualification, this explanation of the relation between his "pollyanalytics" and his fiction. Is it not possible that the famous "doctrine" antedates both fiction and essay, and receives two different forms of literary expression? Critics have often, and rightly, accused Lawrence of weighing down his fiction with a burden of intrusive, almost propagandistic passages of "philosophy". At the same time, his essays often evince a high imaginative and even poetic vitality, as they focus extensively on mother, child, lover, and beloved – concrete figures of his fiction. Unpoetic, unconcrete, "essayistic" preaching may well be defined as an inevitable toll exacted for the larger and more artistic portion of this fiction. The interminable digressions of Rupert

---

[1]   D. H. Lawrence, *Fantasia Of The Unconscious*, 1922 (New York, 1960), p. 57.

Birkin, for instance, suggest that Lawrence's doctrine may not have been so much "deduced" from the novels as decided beforehand, and then *tested* in the fiction. In short, the relation between novels and doctrine may be more complicated than D. H. Lawrence pretends. Yet precisely because of such complications, precisely because doctrinal abstraction and dramatic concretion typically and bewilderingly intermesh in Lawrence's work as a whole, his essays and novels often cast upon each other a reciprocal light, and readily lend themselves to comparisons which reveal the underlying unity of Lawrence's poetic intuition and his philosophic thought. It is because of this reciprocal relationship that my discussion of *The Rainbow* does not limit itself to the doctrine contained in the novel. That limitation is always artificial.

But Lawrence provides a more basic justification for interrelating doctrine and fiction, meaning and form, or what I call "psychology" and "rhythm". The rhetoric of all his writing insists on the moral necessity for this connection. He claimed "it was the greatest pity in the world, when philosophy and fiction got split."[2] Lawrence's work represents a sustained effort to combine the *élan* of the artist with the Word of the prophet. Indeed, it was the gospel word to him, and any attempt to treat Lawrence as a secular artist does his fictional method and doctrinal vision a great injustice. "It seems to me", Lawrence says, "that even art is utterly dependent on philosophy; or if you prefer it, on a metaphysic that governs men at the time and is by all men more or less comprehended and lived."[3] What Lawrence surely recognizes here is that *all* good art is governed by something very like religious ends. What distinguishes Lawrence is the particular quality of his religion, the evangelical tone of his exhortation, and the dogmatic rejection of the spurious split between his religion and other aspects of his work. Fortunately, since the mid-fifties the

[2] D. H. Lawrence, "Surgery For The Novel – Or a Bomb", in *Phoenix: The Posthumous Papers of D. H. Lawrence*, 1936. Edward D. McDonald, editor. (New York, 1936), p. 520.
[3] *Fantasia*, p. XV.

simplistic critical habit of dividing Lawrence into aesthetic and prophetic halves virtually has ceased – but only to the extent that the division is not primarily evaluative. There is no longer the critical craze to damn the doctrine and praise the fiction, but there is still reticence to show the very *specific* connections between them. That is, it used to be a truism in Lawrentian criticism that the artist in him miraculously survived despite the sententiousness, redundancy, or plain stupidity of the Lawrence credo. Mark Spilka was one of the first critics to talk in a persuasively integrated fashion about "whole knowledge" in Lawrence, about the implications that all his work was governed by "religious ends". Spilka explains how in his creative work as well as in his sermons and pronouncements Lawrence wanted to "inform and lead into new places the flow of our sympathetic consciousness".[4] This terminology is echoed by Lawrence in his study of Hardy, as he refers to his own work as a "religious effort . . . to conceive, to symbolize, that which the human soul, or the soul of the race, lacks, that which it is not, and, which it requires, yearns for".[5] Although this syntax is painful, the key words are "conceive", "symbolize", "requires", and "yearns for". The sense of this passage is illustrated in the meaning of form in *The Rainbow*. *The Rainbow* is, as I shall attempt to illustrate, a meticulously planned three-stage process that uses the symbol of the womb after conception as a metaphor for the human race's necessary striving for a birth to unfettered freedom and organic wholeness. Because the psychology of this development, *and* its metaphorical equivalent, are enunciated in Lawrence's "pollyanalytical" essays, and because this embryonic development is the basis of the rhythmic patterns in the novel, a discussion of the psychology of rhythm in *The Rainbow* is a convenient means of closing the gap between form and content in a treatment of Lawrence.

---

[4] Mark Spilka, *The Love Ethic of D. H. Lawrence* (Bloomington, Indiana, 1953), p. 3. The last quotation in the sentence Spilka quoted from *Lady Chatterley's Lover*, chapter 9.

[5] D. H. Lawrence, "Study of Thomas Hardy", in *Phoenix*, p. 447.

For the gap has not really closed. It is still fashionable to discuss the relationship between Lawrence's art and prophecy only in the most general of ways. Mark Spilka talks brilliantly but not comprehensively about a "love ethic" in the major fiction of Lawrence which he justifiably believes relates to a vision of life evident throughout his work.[6] F.R. Leavis with characteristic bravado claims that Lawrence's novel form and visionary message combine to place him somewhere in the great tradition of the English novel.[7] Alan Friedman goes beyond Leavis to explain how Lawrence's use of what Friedman calls the "open-ending" in two of his novels results from the logical extension, not just of the thematic and formal concerns in each novel, but of the controlling art and vision in all of Lawrence's writings.[8] I mention these three critics in particular because they best represent the reversal of the dangerous tendency to over-emphasize Lawrence's doctrine or biography (cf. Murry, *Son of Woman*[9]), or to pigeon-hole him as an aesthetic primitive, or "symbolist", (as William Y. Tindall[10] and others have done), as if the body of Lawrence's religion does not make clear how unfortunately reductive these positions are. But I believe that even the best of the revisionist critics have not gone far enough in their attempt at "whole" criticism. If we take their intelligent emphases to conclusion it should be possible not only to show general relationships between an ethic of love and a novelist's development, or between the tradition of English fiction and Lawrence's own unconventional contribution to it, or even between open-endings in novels and philosophical systems. But also it should be possible to prove the very specific connections between Lawrence's vision of life and an individual novel, or between the principles of his psychology and the rhythmic patterns of verbal, symbolic, and broadly structural repetition in the novel itself. Thus if

---

[6] Mark Spilka, *The Love Ethic of D. H. Lawrence.*
[7] F. R. Leavis, *D. H. Lawrence: Novelist* (London, 1955).
[8] Alan Friedman, *The Turn of the Novel* (New York, 1966).
[9] J. Middleton Murry, *D. H. Lawrence: Son of Woman*, 1931 (London, 1954).
[10] William York Tindall, ed., *The Later D. H. Lawrence* (New York, 1952).

Lawrence's work is as "whole" as Father Tiverton[11] and Mark Spilka first suggested, an extended discussion of one novel can indicate how emphatically Lawrence's fiction lives his vision of life. My study attempts to do this by studying the relationship between D. H. Lawrence's fundamental psychology and the form of *The Rainbow*. It is an attempt to clarify simultaneously the function and interrelationship of rhythm and the meaning of the psychology in that novel. I do not attempt any comprehensive study of Lawrence's ideas about psychology. I deal only with those basic "pollyanalytical" principles that are most helpful in a discussion of form and meaning in *The Rainbow*. My discussion is directed not towards meaning *and* form in the novel, but the meaning of form – that is, the psychology of rhythm. This is the meaning which is best understood by noting the interrelationship between the aesthetic intention of the novelist and the vision of life which for Lawrence governs that intention.

My definition of rhythm is quite simple, and it takes its cue primarily from E. K. Brown's discussion of it in *Rhythm in the Novel*,[12] and secondarily from E. M. Forster's brief treatment of rhythm in *Aspects of the Novel*.[13] I shall use their terminology and consider rhythm as "repetition with variation", a repetition which makes for a unifying order in a novel. Brown states: "Between exact repetition and unlimited variation lies the whole area of significant *discourse* and significant *form*" (my italics).[14] It is precisely the functional interrelationship within this area of "discourse" and "form" that I stress in my consideration of the psychology (i.e., the meaning, the discourse) of rhythm (i.e., the form) in *The Rainbow*. I shall show, to use Brown's terminology, how the rhythmic arrangement of phrases, character gradations, incidents, "expanding" and "fixed" symbols, and interweaving themes "uni-

---

[11]   Father William Tiverton [William Robert Jarrett-Kerr], *D. H. Lawrence and Human Existence* (New York, 1951).
[12]   E. K. Brown, *Rhythm In the Novel* (Toronto, 1950).
[13]   E. M. Forster, *Aspects of the Novel* (New York, 1958).
[14]   Brown, p. 8.

fies and intensifies" the meaning of life that Lawrence wishes to convey and the form that conveys the meaning. The rhythmic use of gradation in character is reflected in *The Rainbow* by the significant differences and similarities between the three central pairs of men and women in the novel. The interweaving theme, which is expressed through the gradation in character, concerns an escape to freedom and the struggle for birth that each generation of male and female Brangwens undergoes. In this sense Lawrence's use of this theme conforms to Forster's belief that the interweaving theme depends mainly on a relationship between the larger parts of a novel: in *The Rainbow* the larger parts are the separate generations. By "fixed symbol" I mean a symbol that is, in Forster's graphic term, a "banner" – a symbol that remains virtually unchanged throughout the novel, and is evoked always with the same meaning. The fixed symbols in *The Rainbow* are the womb and the arch. Associated with the fixed symbol is the "expanding symbol" of the rainbow, a symbol for the complete organic birth that Lawrence desires. It is, literally, an expanding symbol in this novel for it relates to the gradual metaphorical expansion of the womb that will culminate in the birth of a new individual. The rainbow is an expanding symbol because it accretes greater meaning as the novel progresses, and although it ultimately is seen in full, it is never revealed in its full meaning even on the last page of the novel, when it appears for the final time. Brown's suggestion about expanding symbols in general works for the rainbow in particular: the rainbow has different significance for different characters, and a response to it becomes "an index to value in a character".[15] Within the rhythmic rise and fall of generations in *The Rainbow* (cf. Forster on the rhythm in *War and Peace)* similar and dissimilar people confront essentially the same problem of birth, and only gradually will the rainbow symbol reveal itself as the goal of the confrontation. Brown writes in *Rhythm in the Novel:*

[15] Brown, p. 51.

By the slow uneven way in which it accretes meaning from the *succession of contexts* in which it occurs, by the mysterious life of its own it takes on and supports; by the part of its meaning that even on *the last page of the novel* it appears still to withhold – the expanding symbol responds to the impulses of the novelist who is aware that he *cannot give us the core of his meaning,* but strains to reveal now this aspect of it, now that aspect, in a *sequence* of sudden flashes. (p. 57, my italics)

It is as if Brown wrote this passage with *The Rainbow* in mind. It is the succession of sudden flashes, of compromised versions of the rainbow symbol that relate to the birth motif which forms the basic rhythm of the novel. And when the rainbow does appear on the last page, it still provocatively withholds answers to questions I will raise shortly. Finally, all of Lawrence's writings emphasize that the "core" knowledge of any meaning is deathly, and to seek for the core of real "life-knowledge" (i.e., birth) is to seek for what is properly unobtainable.

Implicit in the relatively slight concern about a specific and integrated analysis of form and content in Lawrence's fiction is the widespread belief that Lawrence at his most repetitious moments, in his moods of heated insistence on particular phrases, symbols, or advice, has lost control of his "art". And unfortunately, occasionally the belief holds true: Rupert Birkin nags too much in *Women In Love,* "will" is mentioned too often in the teaching experience of Ursula in *The Rainbow,* and there are numerous other instances in his fiction of disturbing adjectival dogmatism and harmfully intrusive polemicizing. But usually the very repetition of doctrine is intimately related to the full meaning of the passage, and this meaning is expressed in the personal but provocatively aesthetic terms that articulate prophets with private visions and symbols frequently possess. Lawrence does repeat himself constantly, whether it is a phrase, symbol, or situation. However, this repetitive rhythm of Lawrence's novels is part of his vision of life. It is not only necessary to his meaning, it is the form his meaning must take to be true to the repetitive rhythmic form of life. Lawrence states in the Foreward to *Women In Love:*

In point of style fault is often found with the continual slightly modified repetition. The only answer is that it is natural to the author, and that every natural crisis in emotion or passion or understanding comes from this pulsing, frictional, to-and-fro which works up to culmination.[16]

The phrase "continual, slightly modified repetition" is Lawrence's version of Brown's definition of rhythm as "repetition with variation". The "natural crises" which Lawrence mentions so defensively create the repetition in *The Rainbow* that is at the heart of the rhythmic structure of that novel. This rhythmic pulsing toward consummation is most evident, naturally, in the many scenes of sexual exchange in the novel; then the working toward climax has an obvious stylistic significance that cannot be separated from the "physiology" it describes. But for Lawrence the rhythm of any natural crisis is also the microcosm of the lengthy major and *continuing* crisis in a person's life which also "works up to culmination": a person's "passionate struggle into conscious being"[17] – his emergence from a devitalized state of being into a birth to organic wholeness. A struggle into conscious being is the birth that Lawrence unparadoxically insisted must be predicated on the spontaneous, complete realization of the *unconscious* impulses that arise in what he aptly called the "creative unconscious" of each individual. The unconscious is creative, quite simply, because its realization creates a human being, as it permits him to be "born". In his *Letters* Lawrence says that "we must grow from our deepest underground roots – out of the unconsciousness, not from the conscious concepts which we falsely call ourselves".[18] In *Psychoanalysis and the Unconscious* he deals with the same subject: the unconscious "is the active, self-evolving soul bringing forth its own incarnation and self-manifestation . . . the true, pristine unconscious in which all

---

[16] D. H. Lawrence, *Women In Love*, 1920 (New York, 1960), p. viii.

[17] A phrase first used specifically in the Foreward to *Women In Love*, p. viii, but it is applicable to the situations described in most of his better fiction.

[18] *The Collected Letters of D. H. Lawrence*, edited by Harry T. Moore (New York, 1962), p. 396.

our genuine impulse arises...."[19] The design of *The Rainbow* is an exhaustive effort to follow an actual incarnation – the organic Word made flesh in the person of Ursula.

Lawrence believes that this common "pulsing to-and-fro" in his novels is a basic rhythmic pattern in life that he reflects in the design of art itself:

Design in art is a recognition of the relation between various things, various elements in the creative flux. You can't *invent* a design. You recognize it, in the *fourth dimension*. That is, with your blood and your bones, as well as with your eyes.[20]

Thus it is the nature of these "elements" in creative flux to establish interrelationships, and these relationships lead to the crises that are reflected in an "uninvented" pulsing, sensuous rhythm of prose. As an introductory example of what Lawrence means both by considering design in art as a relationship between various elements, and what he means by the use of rhythmic repetition in crisis, I quote four passages from *The Rainbow*:[21]

The rhythm of the work carried him away again, as she was coming near ... there was a swish and hiss of mingling oats, he was drawing near.... He worked steadily ... nearer and nearer to the shadowy trees.... And she was coming near ... and ever the splash of his sheaves beat nearer (pp. 118–119).

He sheltered her, and soothed her, and caressed her, and kissed her, and again began to come nearer, nearer (p. 229).

She was excited, and unused. Her ... was working nearer, stooping, working nearer.... He came near (p. 219).

But they were going to be near.... She went on, drawing near.... She must draw near ... She knew she dare not draw near (pp. 486–488).

I purposefully have quoted out of context and even left out words to omit any mention of who is involved in each scene. The fact that various people *could* be involved is important for the point I wish to make. In the first passage Will is piling hay

[19] D. H. Lawrence, *Psychoanalysis And The Unconscious*, 1921 (New York, 1960), p. 42 and p. 9.
[20] D. H. Lawrence, "Art and Morality", in *Phoenix*, p. 525.
[21] D. H. Lawrence, *The Rainbow*, 1915 (New York, 1961).

with his future wife; in the second Will is attempting to seduce a vulnerable girl; in the third Will and his daughter Ursula are planting potatoes; in the last Ursula is trying to avoid a pack of horses. That there is a "crisis" of emotion in each passage is obvious, as is the sexuality of all the repetition. What is less clear when these passages are taken from the context that precedes them is that their similar rhythm not only can be compared in terms of the identical kind of repetition, but in the specific terms of the psychology of the novel that creates the general pattern to which they all belong. I shall analyze the psychology of the rhythm of scenes like these in the body of this study. It is sufficient to note here that the repetition of "near" does more than indicate that there is an erotic crisis; the similar syntax of these varied crises alerts the reader that these scenes are meant to be counterpointed against each other as part of the "design in art [that] is a recognition of various elements in the creative flux". And the "various" elements cannot be missed: a boy and his girlfriend; a man and a pick-up; a man and his daughter; a young woman and horses. And the implications of the sexuality in each scene – "felt in the blood and bones" – is describable, and usually *predictable* in terms of the psychology of other rhythms elsewhere in the novel: the rhythmic use of a barn, electricity, flowing, a man in shadow, an arch, and naturally, the total struggle for birth.

Because there is an underlying vision of life that unifies and informs all of Lawrence's work, my study of basic psychological patterns emphasizes two "pollyanalytical" essays of Lawrence, *Psychoanalysis and the Unconscious* and *Fantasia of the Unconscious,* in addition to the principles evident in *The Rainbow*. I occasionally use other Lawrence essays, letters, and fiction to clarify the psychology of rhythm in this novel. I have limited my discussion of his fiction to *The Rainbow* for a number of reasons. First, I want to indicate in great detail the ease in which form and content merge in Lawrence's work. As one of his two best novels, *The Rainbow* seemed a likely choice for this assignment. Second, the rise and fall of generations, as Brown and Forster correctly indicate, makes the isolation of rhythmic patterns more obvious, and I believe my findings prove the validity of their point. Third, the length and complexity of this novel make it suitable for the intensive treatment I feel is necessary. I find that the critical interpretation that results from a study of this kind is radically different from the criticism I have read, much of which seems to me incorrect. My analysis of the psychology of rhythm in this novel focuses consistently on the male as antagonist and the female as protagonist – which gives *The Rainbow* a provocatively feminine bias. This lack of emphasis is especially surprising in view of the hint Lawrence drops in one of his letters. He mentions that the germ of this novel was "woman becoming individual, self-responsible, taking her own initiative".[22] Also, I disagree with those many critics, such as F. R. Leavis, who consider *The Rainbow* as either an unfinished or chaotic book. My attention to the symmetry of the psychology of the rhythm of birth shows that the ending of this novel receives some of the most unchaotic, elaborate preparation of any novel I know of in English. Lastly, I have limited myself primarily to the psychology of two essays both because they are his only exclusively psychological ones, and because the metaphorical structure of one of them *(Psychoanalysis and the Unconscious)*, and the principles about "purposive being", religion, and sexuality in the other *(Fantasia of the Unconscious)* are significant in the discussion of the meaning of form in *The Rainbow* – that is, of its psychology of rhythm.

B. THE MEANING OF FORM IN *THE RAINBOW*

In *Psychoanalysis and the Unconscious,* Lawrence discusses the relation of the child to its mother, when the child is in the womb and during the early stages after birth. This discussion takes the form of a metaphorically "scientific" treatment of

[22] *Letters,* p. 273.

the feelings that an infant and the individual closest to it in
the family – who in this case is the mother – share with
each other. The description of the development of many kinds
of intimate relationships is significantly prolonged, both in the
essay and in *The Rainbow*. Indeed, the fictional use of the womb
as a metaphor for *any* parent-child relationship is suggested
by the action of the novel. For instance, the confrontations
between Will Brangwen and the young Ursula are stressed in
terms of birth-pains and umbilical connections because the
father usurps, if briefly, the sexual role of the mother. In the
generation before there was a similar, though less exhaustive
rhythmic struggle between Lydia's dual need to free herself of
Tom's influence and to lean on him for security, and between
Tom's dual need to recognize the inviolable "separateness" of
Lydia's life and to regain lost power with Lydia by making his
daughter a lady. Anna and Ursula's first task, as both metaphorical embryos and young children, will be the severance of
the corrosive contacts with their fathers.

The insistent portrayal of Ursula as womb-child is the culmi-
nating and summary use throughout the novel of the inter-
related metaphors that describe the process of birth, and the
struggle of an escape to freedom. The connections between
them in the novel are as logical and persuasive as they are
in the essay, and naturally more dramatic. *The Rainbow* describes the efforts of three generations of Brangwens to be
born – that is, to escape to a meaningful freedom by ridding
themselves of all restrictions to their organic being, and thus
providing for the unhampered expression of their essential
selves. The cyclic, systematic concern with generations and
inherited qualities is one of the few conspicuous concessions
that Lawrence makes to the mid and late Victorian novel. For
unlike the sprawling "generation" novelists of the previous
century, Lawrence regards the periods of natural birth, early
childhood, or young adulthood as mere steps before the most
difficult birth – the "passionate struggle into conscious"
being that Lawrence mentions in his Foreward to *Women In
Love*. Though those formative periods signify the rites of pas-

sage, they are not visualized by Lawrence in the conventional
celebratory terms which progressively relate the individual's
coming of age as a fairly predictable process of maturity
that even can be described with a telephoto lens (i.e., Thacke-
ray's *Pendennis* as an obvious example). In fact, the periods
are not really "visualized" or romanticized at all by Lawrence;
they come under such close analytic scrutiny that the outer
world of countryside and politics are shut out for thirty or forty
pages at a time in *The Rainbow* in favor of an introverted concern with his character's developing consciousness. When
Lawrence writes in his letters, in reference to *The Rainbow,*
that "it is quite different in manner from my other stuff –
far less visualized",[23] he no doubt especially has in mind
chapters like "Anna Victrix" or "They Live At The Marsh",
where the intensity of Lawrence's preoccupation with marital
adjustment precludes for remarkably long stretches the visual
backdrop of scenery, or even the intrusion of other people.
Richard Aldington is misleading when he speaks of *The Rainbow*
as "containing a serenity and leisureliness which are absent
from his first three novels".[24] But the long panoramic
glimpses of the English countryside of *Sons and Lovers* appear
quite rarely after the first chapter of *The Rainbow.* Aldington
confuses the minute analysis of an individual's organic
growth with serenity, and that associated, lengthy three-genera-
tion focus on heterosexual conflict with leisureliness. Again in
his letters, Lawrence writes that he thinks *The Rainbow* is
"really a stratum deeper than ... anybody has ever gone, in
a novel":[25] he not only emphasizes the depth of his analysis,
but also the length of time the reader stays in those inter-
nalized, unvisualized depths. The struggles for birth and adjustment in *The Rainbow* between man and himself or between
heterosexual relations will have an even more claustrophobic
framework in *Women In Love.* In that novel, "philosophical"
narrative intrusion combines with extensive character dissec-

---

[23]   *Letters,* p. 183.
[24]   From Aldington's Introduction to *The Rainbow,* p. vii.
[25]   *Letters,* p. 193.

tion and dialogue to eliminate almost all pure visualization; in fact, Lawrence has to indicate in the Foreward to the novel that although the "novel took its final shape in the midst of the period of war", we must not assume that the lack of political reference precludes a consciousness of the war in each of the characters. Politics plays a minor role in the latter part of *The Rainbow*, but it exists to teach Ursula another lesson she must learn in order to be born.

The metaphor of birth in *The Rainbow* is eminently sensible. Given Lawrence's celebrated vitalistic view of the universe, a view that continually separates both the animate and the inanimate into the "living" or the dead, or the "quick" and the cold – rather than immediately into the good and the bad – it is not surprising that he should describe the attempt to achieve this vitality as a matter of life or death, as a process of birth – which is an absolute graduation into life:

A child isn't born by being torn from the womb. When it is born by natural process that is rupture enough. But even then the ties are not broken. They are only subtilized. (*Fantasia of the Unconscious,* p. 72)

It is the awareness that the ties are subtle, that you need that "stratum deeper", which compels Lawrence to spend uninterrupted pages to show, for instance, what an un-emancipated man undergoes when he brings those ties with him to marriage.

Lawrence believes that the process of gestation is analogous to and no less traumatic than post-natal maturation. But there are levels of birth – or perhaps rebirth would be a less complicated term – that characters can achieve in Lawrence's world. If rebirth is complete, as it is with Ursula, it concludes a long series of "sunderings" from family, friends, job, lover, etc., which a capable and relentless person has undergone:

And the struggling youth or maid cannot emerge unless by the energy of all powers, he can never emerge if the whole mass of the world, and the tradition of love hold him back. (*Fantasia of the Unconscious,* p. 150)

It frequently appears that the Lawrence hero or heroine must fight "the whole mass of the world" and ignore "the tradition of love" to reach the state Lawrence describes as complete organic consciousness. Thus there must be less potent rebirths for people like Tom and Will, or Lydia and Anna, which indicate only their relative adjustment to their previously untenable modes of existence. They provide Lawrence with interesting versions of livable but compromised lives, with rebirths that give them equilibrium but not consummation. In *The Rainbow* the achieved state of being of such people is described narratively with heavily qualified praise, and metaphorically by a clipped symbol: the broken, vague, or incomplete arch rather than the spanning rainbow.

Lawrence most clearly justifies the metaphor of birth, the great scope of his novel, and that characteristic repetitive analysis to which each of the many inter-personal relationships is subjected when he says:

The actual evolution of the individual psyche is the result of the inter-action between the individual and the outer universe. Just as a child in the womb grows as a result of the parental blood-stream which nourishes the vital quick of the foetus, so does every man and woman grow and develop as a result of the polarized flux between the spontaneous self and some other self or selves. (*Psychoanalysis and the Unconscious,* p. 46)

It is sufficient to note here that by "polarized flux" Lawrence means the rhythmic and repetitive ebb and flow adjustment between a person's dual desire to give of himself to others (his sympathetic urge) and to keep to himself (his separatist urge).[26] Too much sympathy usually is translated into a bitter feeling of dependency that leads to the opposite of the sympathetic urge — self-restraint. Similarly, an over-separatist, protective assertion of the self ultimately can lead to a sympathetic attachment, because of the painful loneliness implicit in the totally separatist stance. "Flux", of course, is a key connecting term between the psychology and rhythm in Law-

---

[26]   Lawrence describes this rhythm when he discusses the function of the novel in *Lady Chatterley's Lover* (New York, 1962), p. 146: "And here lies

rence's fiction. Obviously a state of flux cannot be described adequately by showing part of it – each change is functional and important in the total pattern; so the scenes of heterosexual conflict in *The Rainbow* (and his other fiction) have countless and often analogous stages of development. The prose can bulge and then relax very quickly, according to the pitch of passion that is reached, a passion that is dependent on the ever-shifting "polar" needs of a person at a particular moment.

As I indicated previously, Lawrence considers "design in art" as "a recognition of the relation between various things, various elements in the creative flux". Thus the design must indicate proof – which is based, quite simply on whether it is accurate – that the artist has recognized a fact, a "shimmering truth" about the process of life, as Lawrence would say. This definition of Lawrence's significantly emphasizes the priorities in his work: it is the unmistakeable sense of life awareness rather than Jamesian subtlety and finesse in translating the awareness in art that Lawrence considers the most important index to a novel's greatness. Of course the talents need not be mutually exclusive; it is not that Lawrence sophomorically splits form and content so that he becomes the champion of truth at the utter risk of formal disorganisation. He knows that where there is no order there is nothing for the reader to understand. His well-known statement expressing distrust in the artist and faith in the tale[27] is an interesting way of arguing for the approach he feels is most meaningful: if the novelist does not plumb his ego and does not embroider with undue artistic devices his own "gut" recognition of the "relation between various elements in the creative flux", it is

---

the importance of the novel properly handled. It can inform and lead into new places the flow of our sympathetic consciousness, and it can lead our sympathy away in recoil from things gone dead. Therefore, the novel, properly handled, can reveal the most secret places of life: for it is in the *passional* secret places of life, above all, that the tide of sensitive awareness needs to ebb and flow, cleansing and freshening."

[27] D. H. Lawrence, "The Spirit of Place", in *Studies In Classic American Literature,* 1923 (New York, 1964), p. 2.

precisely the unembroidered pattern of this recognition which will provide the adequate design, the form of the novel. It is a sort of vitalist's "argument from design": there is marvelous design in the intricate processes of life, and if you *really* feel the process you can at least approximate the design. It is not that Lawrence refuses to order his felt recognition with all the necessary props that art can provide. But Lawrence would rather be (and he is) repetitious, exhaustive, and even predictable in his descriptions, for instance, of marital battle, than strikingly pungent and elliptical. That is, because Lawrence strives to recognize patterns in the creative flux, and because certain patterns naturally appear in life with little variation, the rhythm of Lawrence's prose and psychology has the truthful, (and hence) frequently repetitive quality of similar sounds and similar truths in very similar situations. The rhythm of art remains true to the recurrent pattern of Lawrence's psychology of life. Thus when just one partner in a heterosexual relationship indulges in a sympathetic transfer which Lawrence wishes to describe in detail, the prose is almost always turgid and heavily metaphorical, and the sentence structure of great length. It is as if the circuits of exchange (and electricity is his key symbol in reference to polarity) are too excited to stop, as they rush headlong into the description of various stages of consummation. Before I turn to the rhythm of the recurrent birth metaphor and to the three generations in *The Rainbow,* I list below three similar instances in which Lydia, Anna, and Ursula establish sympathetic contact with their males; note that each description is in long sentences that are abruptly pulled up when the receiver cannot respond adequately and when the charge of passion is completed:

Her eyes, with a blackness of memory struggling with passion, primitive and electric at the back of them, rejected him and absorbed him at once. But he remained himself. . . . Then again, what was agony to him, with one hand lightly resting on his arm, she leaned forward a little, and with a strange, primeval suggestion of embrace, held him to her mouth. It was ugly-beautiful, and he could not bear it. (p. 40)

As she watched, her face shining and flower-like with innocent love, his face grew dark and tense, the cruelty gathered in his brows, his eyes turned aside, she saw the whites of his eyes as he looked aside from her. . . . But from his body through her hands came the bitter-corrosive shock of his passion upon her, destroying her in blossom. She shrank. (p.178)

It lasted till it was agony to his soul, till he succumbed, till he gave way as if dead, lay with his face buried, partly in her hair, partly in the sand, motionless, as if he would be motionless now forever, hidden away in the dark, buried, only buried, he only wanted to be buried in the goodly darkness, only that, and no more. He seemed to swoon. (p. 479)

As the above passages indicate, Tom Brangwen, Will Brangwen, and Anton Skrebensky successively fall prey to various kinds of over-sympathetic attachments to their wives or lovers. If we use Brown's broad definition of rhythm as repetition with variation,[28] the importance of this pattern of male emasculation is quite apparent. Each male is "hooked" more emphatically than the preceding one, just as the struggle for rebirth of their corresponding females is more prolonged. In fact, the span of Lawrence's description of the relationship between Ursula and Skrebensky is twice the length (almost to the page) of his treatment of the courtship and marriage of Anna and Will — which is twice the length of his description of the Tom and Lydia relationship. This interweaving theme of birth is accompanied throughout the novel by the expanding symbol of the rainbow.

This tripartite structure can be regarded as a series of three concentric and open-ended circles, with the Marsh Canal as convenient connecting point in the center; each circle, in terms of the length it takes to finish it and its proximity to the "unknown" area of birth, is twice the circumference of the circumscribed one; each circle is open-ended because the literal and metaphorical birth of one generation moves even-

---

[28] A good example of repetition *without* variation in *The Rainbow* is the interpolated descriptions of the drowning body of Tom Brangwen. This is the method used in much greater scale in the "Wandering Rocks" chapter of Joyce's *Ulysses*.

tually into that of the other – and only after the similar cycles of psychological concerns that aid or retard the birth have been described with the similar rhythmic use of metaphor, syntax, and incident. The feeling one gets after the first generation is that the sound has been heard before, but the rhythm becomes louder and more drawn-out. The final circle significantly moves out and beyond – the psychology is the same, the achievement unchartered – to celebrate Ursula's completion of a struggle begun really two generations before. Lawrence purposefully entitles two earlier chapters "The Widening Circle", and the final chapter moves *through* and describes the rainbow, the widest arc of all. I do not find the slackening off in the final section that F. R. Leavis and other critics moan about. The novel seems to gain centrifugal force as it twice doubles out on itself until it thrusts a "born" Ursula beyond the final circle to areas that Lydia and Anna could not attain. The final circle excludes all people but Ursula; as it bends toward the open-end in the last chapter, there is no dialogue at all, but only narrative reference almost entirely about her. She stands on the shore of the wide world, but unlike Keats, she is buoyed by her realization of the strength it took to get there.

The expanding symbol of the rainbow, or a version of it, appears at the conclusion of each of the three main sections of the novel, and periodically within each section. Brown explains that an expanding symbol will function the length of the novel and "hold a reader's sense of its inexhaustible beauty" only "if the symbol is given a surplus of meaning."[29] Obviously, the rainbow symbol has a surplus of meaning and inexhaustible beauty because the ideas that it renders – that Ursula is "born", and that a new world is pledged – cannot be isolated from the questions that it raises: What does Ursula's "birth" signify in terms of immediate results for her? What does that brave new "world built up in a living fabric of Truth, fitting to the over-arching heaven" ask of its inhabitants? *Women In Love* answers much of the first question, but surely

[29] Brown, p. 46.

the second one simply points up that fascinating open-ended structure which Friedman discusses so brilliantly in *The Turn of the Novel*. The rainbow symbol stores up a surplus of meaning as it passes through the tripartite structure of the novel not because it comes to stand for so much meaning as the novel progresses, but because it cannot help but absorb a rich ambiguity of so much relevant and possible *associated* concerns up to the moment of Ursula's vision. The possibilities are fascinating, and the resolutions unclear: If Anna were to spurn domesticity, would she have to leave Will as a consequence of her achievement of organic being? Would Lydia have to leave Tom? To what extent can hereditary drawbacks (i.e., a slow mind or weak body) be overcome so that a person can grasp the vision of the rainbow? As though to answer the implications of these questions, Brown further says that "the expanding symbol is a device far more appropriate for rendering an emotion, an idea, that by its largeness or subtlety cannot become wholly explicit."[30] Thus in reference to the rainbow symbol, can any emotion or idea be considered wholly "explicit" if we cannot be sure what the emotion demands or the idea implies? For instance, although we surely sense the emotional ecstasy of Ursula at the end of the novel, that same euphoria is associated (for us and for her) with the idea of the rainbow; the idea of the rainbow, although it symbolizes Ursula's birth, is not finite and neatly encapsulated, but is endlessly suggestive in ways I've tried to indicate. The reader of the novel should find himself in the interesting position of sharing Ursula's optimism, but feeling more uncertain about just where the feeling of hers will lead. Thus the rhythmic use of the expanding symbol is associated with the tentative final judgments that can be made concerning the ideas suggested by the rainbow. It is this tentativeness about the final "answers" about life that Lawrence considers fundamental in a philosophy that proclaims it is "the first business of every faith to declare its ignorance" *(Fantasia of the Unconscious,* p. 62), and in *The Rainbow,* which asks

[30] Brown, p. 56.

more than once: "And always the way of love would be found. But whither did it lead." The end result must remain vague, but the struggles for birth and freedom in each of the three generations is quite clear and open to analysis.

2. THE RHYTHM OF EMASCULATION AND INCOMPLETE BIRTH

A. INITIAL LABOR: TOM AND LYDIA

Tom Brangwen is an adolescent even in his twenties. He is the naive, pampered youngest son of a matriarchal household in a
cloistered rural area called the Marsh. He has all the physical-
electricity that Lawrence deems so important (perhaps the first
writer not to be *ultimately* condescending about brute sensual
charisma), but none of the bedrock experience that would, in
terms of *Sons and Lovers,* turn this "warmth into intensity like a
white light". He goes to Lydia without meeting a Miriam first, and
he never burns too brightly after that. Tom's struggle for freedom, for organic consciousness, is related to the familiar battles that insecure youth wages for satisfactory socio-sexual adjustment. As so often happens to the unready adolescent, Tom
compounds the dangers of his ingenuousness by marrying before his birth into self-secure manhood. Lawrence's own life, in
fact, is dramatic proof of the insistence that this "readiness" is
so important a consideration in establishing a marriage: in his
letters he frequently notes his own completed arc of maturity,
regards with understanding Frieda's dissatisfaction with her
marriage, contemplates their intense feelings for each other, and
quite unhesitatingly (he doubts *nothing*) takes a mother from
her husband and children. You pay a price in Lawrence's world
if you marry to be born; indeed, the marriage can stabilize,
comfort, and apply stimulus to what Lawrence calls a man's
"sense of purpose", but for full freedom the man must be
father to the marriage. In all of Lawrence's fiction, only Rupert

Birkin, Ursula Brangwen, Mellors, and the Man Who Died conform to this simple rule – and, of course, the Man had to literally die to be born.

Though in his mid-twenties when he marries Lydia, Tom's personal history is conspicuously free of the scars from pubic wars of initiation which Lawrence describes in *Fantasia of the Unconscious:*

> Pull him [the boy] through some narrow aperture, to be born again, and make him suffer and endure terrible hardships, to make a great dynamic effect on the consciousness, a terrible dynamic sense of change in the very being. In short, a long, violent initiation, from which the lad emerges emaciated, but cut off forever from childhood, entered into the serious, responsible pale of manhood. (p. 147)

With this archetypal emphasis[1] on "narrow aperture" (the opening to the unknown), "terrible hardships", "violent initiation", and "pale of manhood", Lawrence sounds like the colorful primitivist he so often is loosely described as. I might note, however, that with the sexual revolution in the past twenty years, and with the associated resurgence of the experiential, behaviorist schools of psychology (which, incidentally, base their therapy on a less scientific stress on the acceptance of certain rhythms of life), Lawrence moves more easily into the mainstream of current socio-psychological thought; his stress on the ultimately positive effects of the rhythm of the life experience (even if the experience is "terrible"), and his demand for obliterated apron strings of any kind between parent and child – all this is basic in his idea of the most stable foundation for future sexual adjustment and marital success.

The "emergence" that Lawrence mentions in the above passage from *Fantasia of the Unconscious* is chronicled in *Sons and Lovers,* when an emaciated and deracinated Paul is reborn as he follows the faint glow into the city of man on the last page of the novel. His brother William did not even emerge emaciated, but wasted away under the pressures of a premature and un-

---

[1] Philip Rieff's book, *The Triumph of the Therapeutic* (New York, 1966) is very helpful for understanding the relationship of Lawrence's psychology to Jung's and Freud's.

healthy attachment to a silly, predatory girl. This emergence motif categorically splits off all of Lawrence's fictional men into the men and boy-men, with people like Skrebensky, Rico, Gerald, and Clifford even coming close to a cringing babyhood. Unlike Paul and William Morel, Tom Brangwen is full-muscled and healthy when he concludes courtship; but this is because his life has "emerged" nowhere, as he takes an unhealthy chunk of his childhood with him to Lydia Lensky's bed, and thereby insures a heavily qualified birth for himself.

A brief summary of Tom's early life indicates the frequency of Lawrence's use of the symbol of freedom, and the extent to which the necessary severance from youth and proper initiation is absent in Tom. After a predictably unhappy sexual experience with a prostitute, Tom feels shame because "he could not get free" of his thoughts of women. It is a familiar syndrome in life and in Lawrence's fiction: the frightened Tom introverts the encounter and makes it count in his mind only as so much attempted and so much failed. Lawrence talks of this kind of bondage in the context even of a happy marriage when he writes in his letters: "It is the hardest thing in life to get one's soul and body satisfied from a woman so that one is free from oneself."[2] By "free from oneself" Lawrence means free from the need to relate satisfaction of the self only in terms of egotistical achievement and personal preoccupation. It is freedom not likely to be felt when an insecure person feels a need to prove himself through a sexual adventure. Failure would intensify his sense of inferiority and success do nothing except imprison him in a life that always looks for more meaningful situations to reinforce this superficial sense of achievement.[3] Thus Tom Brangwen turns to alcohol, periodically drinks himself into a stupor, but still finds that "he could not get free" (p. 22). When the quantity of liquor finally calms him, Lawrence is quick to add that "he had achieved his satisfaction by obliterating his own individuality, that which it depended on

---

[2] *Letters,* p. 251.
[3] "Sex is not living till it is unconscious: and it never becomes unconscious by attending to sex." *Letters,* p. 374.

his manhood to preserve and develop" (p. 23). In terms of *Fantasia of the Unconscious,* Tom thus substitutes the short-range effects of an artificial stupor (none of that "dynamic sense of change" or "long, violent initiation") to burn out the youth from his blood. This does not mean that his attraction for Lydia is superficial, but it guarantees that the very "otherness" of her that attracts him ultimately will intimidate his own unborn soul; unable to feel his own freedom, he can neither understand or recognize the inviolable freedom of others.

But the infatuating early stages of relationships do have their beneficially purging results. When Tom meets Lydia, her self-possession excites him, as he finds that "she set him curiously free" (p. 31). "Free" because she inspires him to a confidence that breaks the circle of his own egocentric worries – the circle image moves out slightly – and "curious" because such a feeling is quite unknown to him. As he dwells on her and warms to the idea of life with her, he significantly is described as "a creature evolving to a new birth" (p. 34). Then the inexperienced Tom unsurprisingly begins also to fear the strange demeanor of Lydia, and the birth metaphor completely disappears; when he senses the challenge she represents to his own chaste being, pure fear stimulates his desire for her as much as sensual passion – and men are not "born" on the heels of such contradictory emotions. At Tom's moment of decision Lawrence quietly rephrases a platitudinous line in a provocative way: "And then it came upon him that he would marry her and she would be his *life*" (p. 35, my italics). "Life" – not the expected phrase "wife" – for the substitution indicates the quality of Tom's error. He retards his birth to freedom and reflects his own stillborn development by picturing marriage as the prerequisite rather than the *after-function* of proud, complete malehood. Very much in character, he is like the wide-eyed, insecure adolescent whose organic priorities become confused in the excitement of courtship. He predicates his potency in the world strictly on the slim foundation of his relationship with her: "He must, in the starry multiplicity of the night, humble himself, and admit and know that without her he was nothing. He was nothing. But with her he would be real" (p. 35). When after years of marriage Tom is described as dissatisfied because all he has known was "the long marital embrace with his wife" (p. 124), Lawrence has translated into dramatic terms the result of not heeding the admonition that he makes many times in his non-fictional writings:

When man loses his deep sense of purposive, creative activity, he feels lost and is lost. When he makes the sexual consummation the supreme consummation, even in his *secret* soul, he falls into the beginnings of despair. When he makes woman, or the woman and the child the great centre of life and life-significance, he falls into the beginnings of despair. (*Fantasia of the Unconscious*, p. 143)

It is interesting to note that Tom's marriage to Lydia is not one of "despair" but generally of a dull, bovine contentment which is interrupted by periods of unhappiness, the origin of which Tom can sense but characteristically cannot quite put into words:

Was his life nothing? Had he nothing to show, no work? He did not count his work, anybody could have done it. . . . He lay with his wife in his arms, and she was still his fulfillment, just the same as ever. And that was the be-all and the end-all. Yes, and he was proud of it.   (p. 124)

The rhythm of Lawrence's prose here is disarmingly leisurely, structurally quite simple – indeed, almost childishly dull – just as the logic of Tom's justification is ultimately evasive (he is not all that "proud") and of the protest-too-much variety that young boys feel when they rationalize rather than admit their error. But Tom's defense mechanisms work for him because he is provided with luxuries of the purposeless eunuch: he is more often content than unhappy in his marriage because he can never feel the despair of losing what he once had, for he *never had it*. In the best and worst of senses his wife is his best part. He cannot feel that he has lost part of his foundation for creative activity because unlike Will, Skrebensky, and Gerald (all of whose bases for living are suspect but still rigidly *there*), Tom went into marriage in a rather purposeless state, with no previous *raison d'être*. Will Brangwen witnesses the destruction of many of his cherished beliefs in the church. Ursula Brangwen annihilates the petty Benthamite basis of Anton Skrebensky's existence and nearly kills him. Gudrun Brangwen does kill and emasculate Gerald Crich by making him realize that *she*, and not the mines, is the necessary rock for Gerald to build his impotent life upon.

Thus all three men – Will, Skrebensky, and Gerald – in various ways, discover that they cannot really function effectively outside the orbit of their women; and their awareness of the constricting nature of this circle either hampers, frightens, or kills them. Tom, however, goes into marriage willing to compromise his freedom (to him, of course, there is no awareness of compromise) with the belief that his wife Lydia and his daughter Anna are more than sufficient for him; that they will let him feel "free". He significantly proposes to Lydia with the central metaphor of the novel, and with the word that weighs most heavily on his own mind: "You are free – aren't you?" (p. 39). She delays her response, and then answers that she is "free to marry". The answer sounds like a qualification of Tom's question. It is Lawrence's way of reminding us of an added problem in this proposed marriage: Lydia's birth to freedom has not occurred at the time of the proposal. After Tom embraces her when she virtually accepts the proposal, Lawrence writes: "He returned gradually, but newly created, as after a gestation, a new birth in the womb of darkness" (p. 41).

Thus every critical event in Tom's history – from his episode with the prostitute, to his infatuation with Lydia, to his one-line proposal – is described with the related metaphors of birth and escape to freedom. In Brown's terminology of rhythm, they are the "fixed symbols" that are plotted with great frequency around the "expanding symbol" (which I discuss later) of the rainbow. But whether we use terms like "concrete reality", "organic", or "constitutive" (cf. Dorothy Van Ghent, Mark Spilka, and Eliseo Vivas respectively)[4] to describe it, Lawrence's

---

4 In Dorothy Van Ghent, *The English Novel: Form and Function* (New York, 1961); Mark Spilka, *The Love Ethic of D. H. Lawrence;* Eliseo Vivas,

best symbology is peculiarly literal as well as symbolic. It conveniently combines the prophetic value of his psychology with the sense of rhythm that he has as artist. That is, a struggle for freedom and birth is not only a helpful analogue for Tom's early life – it *is* that life itself.[5] Lawrence insists that his characters' post-natal birth pains are more real than imaginary or glibly symbolic; the struggle that they signal is a primary condition of life. Surely all novelists have that minimal psychological insight to understand that youth, broadly speaking, is the period of a person's long battle to become a man; but Lawrence's unqualified commitment to the achievement of organic being explains his radical belief, dramatized in his fiction, that all successful battles are embryonic stages before nothing less than rebirth.

In reference to Lydia, her charismatic aloofness, so attractive and terrifying to Tom, is not merely the result of an inevitable awkwardness in a foreign country. She was stillborn in her first marital experience, and the memories of the pain of her previous marriage color her vision of the future with Tom Brangwen:

The first pangs of this new parturition were so acute, she knew she could not bear it. She would rather remain out of life, than be torn, mutilated into this birth, which she could not survive. (p. 49)

Lydia had served her first husband not as a wife but as a servant. He lived and died oblivious of her, and now, with Tom, she understandably hesitates to initiate a giving, "sympathetic" circuit; she fears that once again the exchange will be one-sided, with her on the burnt-out end. Later, less traumatized and more confident, she meets Tom again, and the pains become more intense and the rhythm of embryonic struggle more pronounced as the sexual connections tighten between her and Tom:

She looked at him, at the stranger who was not a gentleman, yet who insisted on coming into her life, and the pain of a new birth strung

---

D. H. Lawrence: The Failure and The Triumph of Art (Evanston, 1960).
[5] "For the mass of people, knowledge *must* be symbolical, mythical, dynamic ... symbols must be true from top to bottom." *Fantasia*, p. 113.

all her veins to a new form. . . . A shiver, a sickness of new birth passed over her.   (p. 34)

"Strung all her veins to a new form" – Lawrence's metaphor of rebirth could not be more precise: the arteries of communication within Lydia's body will be restructured to permit the sympathetic flow that has been dammed up since the death of her husband.

Thus the lines of their marital discord are predictable. Tom marries a woman before he is a man. He centers his life on his wife's inexperienced shoulders (she formerly had depended on her Polish husband entirely), and he resents any exertion of her "otherness", her need for separateness. Tom characteristically believes that the "unknown" or "strange" quality about her is proof that she will leave him. His childish lack of strength is very clear:

How could a man be strong enough to take her, put his arms around her and have her, and be sure he could conquer this awful unknown next his heart. . . . He must always turn home, wherever his steps were taking him, always to her, and he could never quite reach her, he could never quite be satisfied, never be at peace, because she might go away.   (pp. 53, 55)

It is precisely because an undeveloped Tom Brangwen does not understand that this "awful unknown" of Lydia's is inviolable that he finds after marriage, as the terminology reasserts itself, that "he could not get free" (p. 52).

There is a fascinating scene that indicates the unfortunate extent to which Tom is intimidated by that which he cannot understand, or dominate as food for his egotism. He has just returned from the familiar room where he spent his childhood, after he has put Anna to bed. He then goes to his pregnant wife's room, and a yawning void opens:

He went down to her room entering softly. She was lying still, with eyes shut, pale, tired. His heart leapt, fearing she was dead. Yet he knew perfectly well she was not. He saw the way her hair went loose over her temples, her mouth was shut with suffering in a sort of grin. She was beautiful to him – but it was not human. He had a dread of her as she lay there. What had she to do with him? She was other than himself.   (p. 76)

There is much that is brilliant here: the silent rhythm of slow, short sentences convey the tentativeness of his approach; eyes that are marvelously "shut, pale, tired"; shut eyes that close him out, pale eyes that he never really sees, tired eyes fatigued by him – all adjectives send out implications he surely senses standing by the door; the joy and ache of childbirth caught in that suffering grin; the very human beauty that he self-protectively considers inhuman because he cannot fathom it. The moment is reminiscent of the final scene in *A Farewell to Arms,* with one most significant difference. Unlike Catherine Barkley, Lydia is a long way from death; she only looks like Frederick Henry's statue to Tom, and the only way he can "make it good" (as Hemingway would say) is to divorce that kind of beauty from the human world of life. Immediately Tom receives the look of recognition from Lydia that makes "a great scalding peace" pass over him. But were Tom stronger, he need not have waited for the look. It is part of the pact of real marriage.

But Lydia must receive a small share of the blame for the marital discord. She too is irritated if she is too obviously made aware of him as a separate power. The remnants of her sympathetic reticence caused by the unhappiness of her last marriage make Lydia unable to rouse Tom out of his chronic fear and inferiority syndrome. Lawrence is aware that an unjealous acceptance of the supreme otherness of your mate is not easy to attain (e.g., the above scene: "she was other than himself"). Above all, it takes compromise, adjustment, and occasional capitulation – you must know when to play the lover and the confidant, and when to leave the beloved in his strange solitude. Though Lydia does not respond to the calls of Tom's insecure soul in a selfless, constructive way, she usually compensates for Tom's immaturity with some receptivity and deft initiative of her own.

A dramatic instance of the contrast between a receptive Lydia and a restrained Tom occurs after she accepts his proposal:

He went very white as he stood, and did not move, only his eyes were held by hers, and he suffered. She seemed to see him with her newly opened, wide eyes, almost of a child, and with a strange movement, that was agony to him, she reached slowly forward her dark face and her breast to him, and with a slow insinuation of a kiss that made something break in his brain, and it was darkness over him for a few moments. He had her in his arms, and, obliterated, was kissing her. And it was sheer, bleached agony to him, to break away from himself. (p. 40)

Note the careful organization of color: "white" and "bleached agony" set off against "darkness" and a "dark face". The scene provides that characteristic Lawrentian conflict between that which is dark, strange and procreative, because beyond the mere "self", and that which is white, bloodless, and reticent, because limited by the ego. Tom does manage to "obliterate" himself briefly, but not without a significant agonizing struggle even to get free enough to receive her kiss. The rhythm of Lawrence's use of incident, metaphor, and syntax is based on the repetition of the psychological patterns he sees in life. Thus after a conversation between Tom and Lydia, the agony and whiteness return with a nearly identical sound:

Then again, what was agony to him, with one hand lightly resting on his arm, she leaned forward a little, and with a strange, primeval suggestion of embrace, held him her mouth. It was ugly-beautiful, and he could not bear it. He put his mouth on hers, and slowly, slowly the response came, gathering force and passion, till it seemed to him she was thundering at him till he could bear no more. He drew away, white, unbreathing.   (p. 43)

Lydia frequently is described as "willing", an "open flower", "unfolded", and "ready to receive"; Tom as "stiffened", "afraid", and "raging". Her usual receptivity, which is more than merely sexual, does contrast with Tom's frequently paralyzed behavior. In short, Tom's childish insistence on dominance and his related self-restraint are more destructive forces on the marriage than is Lydia's occasional coldness. Tom's failure to consummate their relationship before marriage ("he bungled in taking her") provides a preview of their marital difficulties: at that time "she gave herself to the hour" (p. 52), but Tom, unjustly frightened by Lydia's excited attempt to know him as a separate being, postpones the sexual consummation till after their wedding. There is a poignancy about the rhythmic variations on this theme of the inverted (cf. female initiative) sexual war. Witness the sad frustrations of their pre-marital sex, as a lonely and older woman desperately tries to unravel that knot of Tom's insecurity by literally approaching the problem head on:

And then again he was bewildered, he was tied up as with cords, and could not move to her. So she came to him, and unfastened the breast of his waistcoat and his shirt, and put her hand on him, needing to know him.   (p. 52)

Lydia wants to know the separateness of Tom, she wants to feel him in contra-distinction to her the female, she wants to feel his unknowable strangeness as another person. But it is "this other half of devotional love – perfect knowledge of the beloved" (*Psychoanalysis and the Unconscious*, p. 37) to which Tom is scared to submit. After their marriage night Lydia is described again as "coming to life", while he feels increasingly unsure as the morning progresses. This is the "morning-after" post-coital syndrome which is reflected quite similarly in the three heterosexual relationships of the novel. For instance, after their marriage night, Will peevishly objects the next day to Anna's desire to leave his bed and get some food. Like Lydia before her, the sexual exchange has roused Anna to life; and like Tom, Will's life is so centered on his wife that a short absence creates the unfillable void in him. The evening-to-morning rhythm of sex leading to emptiness will receive its climax when Skrebensky knocks on the door of Ursula's room after his midnight destruction and incredibly (because incredulously) asks: "Well, what have I done?" (p. 481).

Tom's fears about Lydia are expressed in a clipped, repetitious syntax that reflects his childish kind of panic:

Did he own her? Was she here for ever? Or might she go away. She was not really his, it was not a real marriage, this marriage between them. She might go away.   (p. 55)

In *Psychoanalysis and the Unconscious*, Lawrence describes how a child, who both fears and desires independence from its parent, has flashes of temper which show how "the little back has an amazing power once it stiffens itself" (p. 23). Lawrence describes how Tom "walked about for days stiffened with resistance to her, stiff with a will to destroy her as she was" (p. 57). Or, in *Fantasia of the Unconscious,* Lawrence mentions "the desire to smash" (p. 80) that a child expresses when it cannot get the love and attention that it wants from the mother. Indeed, Tom is described appropriately in the early stages of their marriage: "He felt he wanted to break her into acknowledgment of him, into awareness of him . . . . He would smash her into regarding him. He had a raging of desire to do so" (p. 59).[6] Or as this rhythm continues into the next generation, Will is frustrated about his previous inability to monopolize the attention of Anna during courtship, and "he wanted to smash through something" (p. 111). And later, Skrebensky's unforgettable crying fit when Ursula tells him she won't marry him is evidence of another tactic that the child-man uses which Lawrence also describes in *Fantasia of the Unconscious:* Lawrence contrasts that crying, with its "insistence on pity" *(Fantasia of the Unconscious,* p. 80), to the "rage" or "smash" pattern that Tom and Will go through. It is as if by the end of the novel, as each woman gets stronger in each generation, the discrepancy between Ursula's and Skrebensky's powers are so great that all the male can do is cry about it and walk away.

After two years of marriage, an exhausted and older Tom Brangwen no longer "shrank from yielding to her" and "he began to flow towards her" (p. 90) – the same immage of flowing movement that Lawrence used earlier for Lydia. This salutary but qualified reconciliation is described in terms of a widening circle, the symbol that Lawrence uses twice as chapter titles during the progress of the next two generations of Brangwens. Most significantly, the circle symbol concludes the first generation's rhythmic pattern of those fixed symbols of birth and freedom, as Tom and Lydia receive their initiation into a safe, stable, and dull life:

---

[6] Lawrence describes him later in the marriage: "He wanted to smash the walls down and let the night in, so that his wife should not be so secure and

Their coming together now, after two years of married life, was much more wonderful to them than it had been before. It was the entry into another circle of existence, it was the baptism to another life, it was the complete confirmation. Their feet trod strange ground of knowledge, their footsteps were lit up with discovery. Wherever they walked, it was well, the world re-echoed round them in discovery. They went gladly and forgetful. Everything was lost, and everything was found. The new world was discovered, it remained only to be explored. (p. 91)

A dull world, of course, because it is never explored, and that is the heavy qualification which Lawrence places on Tom and Lydia's quest for the rainbow condition. Their progress is from fear and constraint to stability and domesticity – fine progress in relative terms, but so much of the absolute is missing. For example, early in the marriage, when he was most intimidated by the justifiable separateness of his wife, Tom was described as "a broken arch thrust sickeningly out from [for?] support" (p. 60). As the marriage progresses, he continues to fear or be excessively humbled by that which he cannot fathom; he turns his back on the unknown rather than show any interest to explore it: "The swift, unseen threshing of the night upon him silenced him, and he was overcome. He turned away indoors humbly. There was the infinite world, eternal, unchanging, as well as the world of life" (p. 76). This awe before the unknown is admirable to Lawrence, but *not* the humble slinking away from it. It is not necessary to throw stones at it like Rupert Birkin (though that is acceptable), but Tom's crippled fascination before the infinite world predictably delimits his potency in the finite world of life. Between the periods of his emasculated, "clipped-arch" condition, and the baptism to another life described above, Tom compensates (just as Will will do) for the strained relationship with his wife by establishing a dangerously sympathetic relationship with his step-daughter Anna. With the achievement of relative stability between Tom and Lydia, Anna is relieved temporarily of her pressures as surrogate wife, and she

---

quiet" (p. 87). And his wife tells him: "You should not want so much attention. You are not a baby" (p. 87).

looks up to see a miniature rainbow that gives her a little room to breathe:

> She was no longer called upon to uphold with her childish might the broken end of the arch. Her father and mother now met to the span of the heavens, and she, the child, was free to play in the space beneath, between.   (p. 92)

Then the freedom metaphor quickly passes to Anna, as "she looked from one to the other, and she saw them established to her safety, and she was free" (p. 92). But "established" and "safety" are the most positive terms that can be applied to this relationship. Tom can grow and learn to curb his insecurities and his related fears of the unknown, but surely he lacks the depth to undertake the sunderings and exploration of an Ursula. Like Aaron Sisson of *Aaron's Rod,* his marriage at an unready hour quenches the unsatisfied questings of his purposive being; and unlike Aaron, he is not the person to make a clean break with his wife and start again. Even the stronger Lydia gives up any attempt to rouse her husband to exploration, as she satisfies herself (as Anna will do) with the puerile discovery of domestic contentment: "Mrs. Brangwen went on in her own way, following her own devices. She had her husband, her two sons, and Anna. These staked out and marked her horizon" (p. 97). The next generation will try to adjust that mark as it inherits the rhythm of the struggle to be born.

B. PROTRACTED PAIN AND COMPROMISE: WILL AND ANNA

The struggle for the organic birth of Will and Anna is more complicated and exhaustive than that of the previous generation of Brangwens. The psychology of their embryonic development is similar to Tom and Lydia's, and the rhythm, unsurprisingly, is quite familiar in this section of the novel. What is significantly different, however, is both the minute analysis to which their "birth" is subjected, and the related heightened emphasis on many of the rhythmic patterns I have attempted to isolate. The structure of the novel itself becomes a kind of moral index.

Will and Anna are worth more space in *The Rainbow* because they have more depth, more potential for meaningful birth. The battle that they wage against each other, through courtship and into marriage, is not equal. Like her mother before her, Anna has that certain edge which cuts deep into the more susceptible Will; she develops a separatist self-sufficiency before her husband, and she is better able to resist his over-sympathetic behavior.

The rhythmic struggle for their individual birth, with all its attendant fears, restraints, and "polar flows", does not lend itself to the relatively quick compromise established by Lydia and Tom. Their final qualified birth resembles the previous generation's because it also portrays the acceptance of domesticity by the female and limited achievement by the male. Yet this similar criticism about the quality of their birth follows a more lengthy battle that is indicative of Anna and Will's greater complexity and Lawrence's more probing characterization. For instance, it would be inconceivable for the gentle, sensual Tom Brangwen to experience Will's pseudosexual orgasm in the cathedral; but impossible only because the less complicated Tom lacks the sensitivity, the "other-worldliness" to respond to the religious experience at all. And Anna's naked dance of annihilation, for all its blatancy, has that fine element of sophisticated timing which would offend her more restrained Polish mother, and would be beyond Lydia's intuitive imagination.

In this generation Lawrence increases the areas of disagreement between his couple, and multiplies their birth pains and problems. It is as though their versatility, quite simply, gives them more to disagree about. The question of the function of religion is the most obvious additional concern for Will and Anna. They experience three births that correspond to the three plateaus they reach in their relationship. The first birth – naturally, a limited one – is that provided by the marriage itself. The second birth follows the temporary resolution of their "separatist" difficulties, as Will accepts Anna's pointed criticism of his absolutist religious attitude. The third and final birth occurs when Will finally escapes from his dependency on Anna and gives her freedom (her final birth) by developing his "purposive self" in limited but useful outside activity. Each birth, and the metaphorical ontogeny along the way, is marked out consistently by Lawrence's rhythmic use of the expanding symbol of the rainbow, the interweaving theme of a flight for freedom, and predictably similar scenes and syntactical patterns. With these words as preface we can begin to trace the psychology of rhythm in this section of the novel.

Anna Brangwen's problems as an adolescent begin with the realization of the new phase of life: "The child before puberty is quite another thing from the child after puberty. Strange indeed is this new birth, this rising from the sea of childhood into a new being. It is a resurrection which we fear" *(Fantasia of the Unconscious*, p. 140). "New birth", "new being" – but the emphatic birth metaphors do not blind Lawrence to the dangers of Tom's relationship with his daughter. Tom Brangwen is rebuffed by his wife early in their marriage, and he is afraid of her: "So he went out of the house for relief. Or he turned to the little girl for her sympathy and her love . . . . So soon they were like lovers, father and the child" (p. 60). This soft, understated prose need not conceal the dangers of parent and child being "like lovers". Lawrence discusses this syndrome in great detail in his two psychological essays, as he examines the inhibiting effect this kind of a relationship can have on a child. He explains that this "dynamic spiritual incest" can be "more dangerous than sensual incest, because it is more intangible and less instinctively repugnant" *(Fantasia of the Unconscious*, p. 153). According to Lawrence it usually results in the premature arousal of the child's sexual desires.[7] Since she will not relate them to her father because of the inhibitions of the super-ego, she will introvert them and thereby inhibit her sexual activity. Fortunately Anna escapes this inhibiting situation, both because of the opportune timing of Will's arrival, and, more importantly, because she is the "lover" of Tom only for that interval

[7] See Philip Rieff's explanation of this syndrome in his Introduction to *Fantasia of the Unconscious*.

in which he cannot function as a man – that period until "she was no longer called upon to uphold with her childish might the broken end of the arch." That "broken end" symbolizes his general phallic breakdown, and the socio-impotent male in Lawrence's world can decimate his family. When Tom stands erect to hoist his share of the burden he saves his stepdaughter as well as himself.

Anna's attachment to Tom is also not strong enough to damage her birth potential because it follows a long period of resentment toward him that is never completely dissipated. That is, before Anna skirts the dangers of dynamic spiritual incest, she resents the intrusion of her stepfather into her matriarchal household, and she clings to her mother. Tom reaches her, finally (and literally), through one of those characteristic scenes of unconscious communion that are scattered throughout Lawrence's fiction.[8] It is essential *not* to disapprove of Tom as he rips off her clothes – and tears her from her mother's womb – when she stubbornly refuses to get undressed:

And he reached his hand and grasped her. He felt her body catch in a convulsive sob. But he too was blind, and intent, irritated into mechanical action. He began to unfasten her little apron. She would have shrunk from him, but could not. So her small body remained in his grasp, while he fumbled at the little buttons and tapes, unthinking, intent, unaware of anything but the irritation of her. Her body was held taut and resistant, he pushed off the little dress and the petticoats, revealing the white arms. She kept stiff, overpowered, violated, he went on with his task. And all the while she sobbed, choking: 'I want my mother.' (p. 72)

The scene is awesome and brutal: "little apron", "small body", "little buttons", "little dress" – all of it "grasped", "pushed", and "violated" by a father. But it is not perverted and not even "sensual", except in the obvious way that many intimate moments between a father and daughter have the healthy momentum of sexual inter-play. The key phrases in the description are "but he too was blind" and "unthinking"; there is a kind of rape

[8] Mark Spilka is especially good on the significance of communion scenes in the fiction of Lawrence. See *The Love Ethic of D. H. Lawrence.*

here, but the instinctive response and counter-response of both of them should justify Tom's actions as a father and illustrate what Lawrence means in *Fantasia of the Unconscious* when he says:

There should be between the baby and the father that strange, intangible communication, that strange pull and circuit such as the magnetic pole exercises upon a needle, a vitalistic pull and flow which lays all the life plasm of the baby into the line of vital quickening, strength, knowing. And any lack of this vital interchange between father and child, man and child, means an inevitable impoverishment to the infant.   (p. 73)

A "vitalistic pull and flow" is the closest Lawrence will come, in a phrase, to describing the origins of his psychology and the justification for his repeated patterns of rhythm. In this scene an angry father does the "pulling", and the "flow" of the child's sympathies will be redirected towards him and away from her mother.

However, what is less evident, perhaps, is that this scene, like the following barn scene, is not in itself part of that spiritual incest which Lawrence condemns. It is a perfectly understandable, instinctive act of a castrated man towards his stubborn daughter, just as Anna's recoil and screaming for her mother is eminently justified by her "polar" needs at that moment. Yet when we consider that after this scene begins the short period of Anna's unhealthy, wifely attachment to her father, is easy to understand why this explicit derobing scene often is misunderstood as even vaguely incestuous. It calls to mind the misunderstandings about the Paul Morel and Gertrude sleeping scene, a scene which is followed by a longer period of Paul's emasculating attachment to his mother. But to paraphrase Mark Spilka's analysis of the incident in *Sons and Lovers*, in the vitalistic communion between Tom and Anna in *The Rainbow* – as between Paul Morel and his mother – Lawrence shrewdly has marshalled all the desires (i.e., Anna's need for a strong male image) that will cause Anna some brief difficulties at the very moment that he has just affirmed, dramatically, in the derobing scene, the wholesome quality of their father-daughter relationship. That is, in life such scenes must occur; that Tom drowns from this incident and emerges *too close* to Anna is a poignant comment on his own marital insecurity. It is by no means an indication of the incestuous nature of the scene itself: "The flashing interchange of anger between parent and child is part of the responsible relationship necessary to growth" *(Fantasia of the Unconscious,* p. 89). "Necessary to growth" – Lawrence implicitly defends the undressing scene in terms of his birth metaphor, just as he does when he warns against the situation where "the dynamic relation between parent and child may fairly easily fall into quiescence, a static condition" *(Fantasia of the Unconscious,* p. 109). For previous to his undressing of Anna, Tom's relationship with her had been quite static – the pull and flow interchange was not there; Lawrence wants to guard against this "quiescence" because he believes it rules out the polarized exchanges which energize the patterns of life and make possible growth and rebirth. At this point Tom Brangwen lacks the organic being to absorb all the energy he receives from his electric rape of Anna. His purposive self is weak, his relationship with his wife is lopsided, and the wholesome vital charge that Tom and Anna receive from this exchange is nearly the cause for Tom's destructive and permanent need for his daughter. But blame Tom, and not the scene.

A second similar communion scene, also not incestuous in itself, is the insistently rhythmic interlude in the barn, which completes Anna's swing from her mother to her father that was initiated when Tom undressed her:

There was a trickling of water into the butt, a burst of rain-drops sputtering on to her shawl, and the light of the lantern swinging, flashing on a wet pavement and the base of a wet wall. Otherwise it was black darkness: one breathed darkness. He opened the doors, upper and lower, and they entered into the high, dry barn, that smelled warm even if it were not warm. He hung the lantern on the nail and shut the door. They were in another world now. The light shed softly on the timbered barn, on the whitewashed walls, and the great heap of hay; instruments cast their shadows largely, a ladder rose to the dark arch of a loft. Outside there was the driving rain, inside, the softly-illuminated stillness and calmness of the barn. Holding the child on one arm, he set about preparing the food for the cows, filling a pan with chopped hay and brewer's grains and a little meal. The child, all wonder, watched what he did. *A new being was created in her for the new conditions* . . . There was a noise of chains running, as the cows lifted or dropped their heads sharply; then a contented, soothing sound, a long snuffing as the beasts ate in silence. The journey had to be performed several times. There was the rhythmic sound of the shovel in the barn, then the man returned walking stiffly between the two weights, the face of the child peering out from the shawl. Then the next time, as he stooped, she freed her arm and put it round his neck, clinging soft and warm, making all easier.   (p. 74, my italics)

In this scene there is that rhythmic working-up to culmination which Lawrence describes to defend his style. That related "emotional" crisis, as he calls it – around which the rhythm is plotted – involves the birth of a new relationship between father and child, and between the child and the world around her: "A new being was created in her for the new conditions." This scene is a kind of preparation for the equally rhythmic yet explicitly erotic crisis that Anna experiences at night with Will in the barn. The rhythm of the later scene is similar to the scene above, but the psychology of that rhythm, of course, is different. For instance, note the striking similarity in dramatic situation and syntactical development between the last few lines of the barn scene quoted above, with this excerpt from Anna and Will's experience with the sheaves:

Into the rhythm of his work there came a pulse and a steadied purpose. He stooped, he lifted the weight, he heaved it towards her, setting it as in her, under the moonlit space. . . . There was only the moving to and fro in the moonlight, engrossed, the swinging in the silence, that was marked only by the splash of sheaves, and silence, and a splash of sheaves.   (pp. 118–119)

The word "pulse" combined with "a steadied purpose" is interesting, for with its implications of movement, followed by steadying movement, it also applies to the father-daughter situation in the barn. For as Tom and Anna Brangwen feed the cows, there is ample evidence of what Lawrence means when he claims that design in art involves a recognition of various elements in the creative flux, a design that must involve that fourth dimension of sense appreciation felt by the "blood and bones". Indeed, there is that sense of constant movement amidst disparate elements in the barn around Will and Anna. The movement contains a chorus of actions at cross-purposes, for it is included by Lawrence as the rhythmic sound of the greater pattern of the creative flux: the water trickles, then bursts, then sputters – and the rain is driving; the lantern swings and then is hung, and he opens and then shuts the door; there is a flashing and there is a black darkness; the child has spasms and the child is quiet; the barn itself "smelled warm even if it were not warm". There is no conventional attempt to integrate or balance these transitions; only the desire by Lawrence for the reader to recognize the sense of flux, disorder, and the beautiful sound this pulsing pattern makes. This is the kind of "pulsing, frictional to and fro" in life (thus in Lawrence's art) that reaches its climax with the statement of the rhythmic sound of the shovel, and its brief resolution when Tom sits down and arranges the child. The "fourth-dimensional" prose is certainly here, for although not erotic, the scene is no less sensual than that about Will, Anna, and the sheaves. Lawrence orchestrates the scene with Tom and Anna around the sense of sight (light and dark), sound ("calmness", "stillness"), taste ("food for the cows"), smell ("smelled warm") and touch ('holding the child on one arm"). And to add some synesthesia, Lawrence describes how "one breathed darkness" and how "the light shed softly". All senses emerge and intersect as the water drips and builds to the crisis of the barn. The air of potent night darkness and the movements and counter-movements of passion create the breath of life. Lawrence will never write a scene that is more "alive" – in his own unplatitudinous sense of that term. But a father and daughter's mutual appreciation of this life force must not be construed as erotic sublimation.

As my analysis suggested, the parental connection which results from the interlude in the barn does more psychological harm to Tom than to Anna. It is the familiar emasculation syndrome. As Tom feels progessively more estranged from Lydia, he channels what little purposive being (which is the prime male element for Lawrence) he has into the doomed attempt to make Anna "a lady". In this transparent way he tries to decastrate himself by transforming his daughter into what he foolishly feels is the equivalent of manhood. The situation is a convenient summary of Tom: his desire to make Anna superficially sophisticated reflects on his diminishing status with his wife; his willingness to believe that such sophistication is meaningful relates to the childishness I discussed in the first part of this chapter. Fortunately, the worst effect that Tom's sublimation has on Anna is that it makes her feel alienated. She is unable to feel close to her mother because of Tom's sexual urging, and she has ambivalent feelings about her father's methods of molding her into a sophisticate. Rebellion ensues, as she yells at the animals, belittles her friends, and openly scorns the tavern spastic. She returns to the explicit context of the interweaving theme of birth and freedom when she finds her only comfort away from her parents where she is "free of people" (p. 93).

As a "lost generation" waif, she meets the self-contained Baron Skrebensky, and "she felt a sense of freedom near him" (p. 94). What she feels, and for the first time, is the total lack of any demand or expectation placed on her in a relationship with another human being. Content within himself, the Baron has all the armor which befits his organic wholeness. Anna responds to the Baron's livingness, to his blue eyes "full of fire", to "his sharp flinging movements" – in short, to the same qualities she originally finds attractive in the less substantial Will. But Anna sees the Baron rarely, so "she wanted to get away . . . many ways she tried, of escape" (pp. 100-101). She first tries to escape through the adolescent's involvement with the Church, until she rejects the rigid formulations of what should be, in essence, a mystical experience: "The falsity of the spoken word put her off" (p. 101). Throughout his writings Lawrence approves of Anna's pointed objection to religion, an objection based on her dislike of a mental indoctrination that ultimately ignores the passionate religious feelings she experiences. Passion – sexual or otherwise – is closely allied to

religious exaltation for Lawrence; according to him, man must
learn to subordinate his religious and sexual desires (both of
which are "non-purposive") to his desire for purposive activity.

Thus religion and sex, as we shall see in the scene involving
Will and the cathedral, involve similar energies that are chan-
nelled on different but parallel courses. That is, they both can
lead to a kind of orgasm, and the orgasm in both cases is an
insufficient base for a man to build his life upon. It is interesting to note, however, that as a wife, Anna later over-reacts to
Will's thoroughly mystical apprehension of religious significance
when she commits the cardinal Lawrentian sin of emphasizing
knowledge as the key to religious appreciation. Her reversal (a
common one in his fiction) is based on her desire to compensate
for Will's delimiting spirituality. Her error is the result of her
justifiable effort to belittle his mistaken belief that the religious
experience, even if rendered mystically, is an absolute, and not
a form of consummation that only *contributes* to the creation
of a whole man. This theme of the intransigence of one's polar
energies plays an important role in the second half of the novel.
One of the outstanding qualities of Ursula, and a central reason
for her escape from the benumbing psychological patterns of
earlier generations, is her steadfast refusal to accommodate her
organic desires in any way. Her uncompromising attitude, once
she has reached a decision, is intimately associated with the relentless rhythm of "sunderings" that follows Ursula to the end
of *The Rainbow*, and to the completed rainbow symbol.

It is at this stage in Anna's life, as she fights for freedom but
is unable to attain it, that she meets her cousin, Will Brangwen.
Her recollection of an earlier meeting provides the most incisive description of him:

She remembered her cousin Will. He had town clothes and was thin,
with a very curious head, black as jet, with hair like sleek, thin fur.
It was a curious head: it reminded her she knew not of what: of some
animal, some mysterious animal that lived in the darkness under the
leaves and never came out, but which lived vividly, swift and intense.
She always thought of him with that black, keen, blind head. And she
considered him odd.   (p. 102)

All of Will lurks in this description: that subterranean "otherness" reflected in his curious rodent's head; his young life sustained by a spirituality that is "keen", "vivid", yet "blind". He presents the beaked face of a bird on the furry head of a rodent on a body that does not seem there – for his body is not too relevant for the circle of existence he draws for himself. That nervousness and self-possession of his bird-face is underscored again when Will appears in person: "Will Brangwen rose uncertainly. He had golden-brown, quick, steady eyes, like a bird's, like a hawk's, which cannot look afraid. . . . He was hovering on the edge of her consciousness" (p. 104). The false rising of a Phoenix, of course, and Lawrence will capitalize on the metaphor shortly. Anna is entranced (in up-dated Desdemona fashion) by Will's etherialized discussions of religion and church architecture. Her infatuation is understandable if we realize how much of a new life Will represents for her after a childhood restricted by the domesticity of her mother, and the deadening blood-intimacy of her father. Thus Anna feels that "in him she had escaped" (p. 109). But the prison doors have just begun to close.

Yet if Lawrence asserts the escape-to-freedom motif again, he leaves little doubt that it is not the strangeness of procreative darkness that she enters:

It was a curious sensation, to sit next to him. The colour came streaming from the painted window above her. It lit on the dark wood of the pew, on the stone, worn aisle, on the pillar behind her cousin, and on her cousin's hands, as they lay on his knees. She sat amid illumination, illumination and luminous shadow all around her, her soul very bright. She sat, without knowing it, conscious of the hands and motionless knees of her cousin. Something strange had entered into her world, something entirely strange and unlike what she knew. (p. 105)

This passage presents the first of many references to Anna and Will together which emphasize the combined elements of darkness, strangeness, and illumination; it is that last element – the intruding, sterile light – which is one signal of incomplete birth. It is the literal illumination which is always absent, for instance, when Birkin and Ursula are together in intimate scenes, as in the forest. But Will and Anna are convinced that a complete birth is taking place, when only the conventionally limited escape of courtship is what they feel: "Gradually the two young people drew apart, escaped from the elders, to create a new thing by themselves" (p. 110). "A new thing", and Will is so convinced of the potent birth arising from their relationship that he confidently carves a phoenix for Anna. The key scene of Anna and Will together is in the barn, just as it was with Anna and her father; and later in the novel a most significant episode between Will and Anna also involves a similar setting. The consistency of Lawrence's emphasis on education within the barn should not go unnoticed, and neither should it be smirked at with "I told you so" expressions of disdain. There is no reason for Lawrence to repeat approximately the same environment for the critical moments of each generation except the obvious one. The rhythmic process, in its most basic form, is the combination of the repeated and the variable, with the repeated as the ruling factor. As E. K. Brown states: "Repetition, expected and then presented, enforces the idea or the feeling, makes it more emphatic in its resonance."[9] That is, there is a kind of psychic meeting or birth communion which each generation experiences in the barn. The repetition of the location sensitizes the reader to the repetition of the psychic experience – it is not that the barn itself is an integral part of the experience. Our understanding of the significance of the different psychological background and our resulting appreciation of the dramatic importance of each scene in the birth motif is aided by counterpointing it to the scenes that precede and follow it. When a distraught Tom sees Will and Anna kissing, that moment in the familiar half-light floods backward to his own episode with Anna in the barn, which initiated her uncomfortably close relationship with him. It also anticipates the future scene when a similarly insecure Will Brangwen carries Ursula to the barn at night.

[9]   Brown, p. 29.

The scene in which Will and Anna silently are observed by Tom also has the bird imagery, the emphasis on "strangeness", and the tell-tale rays of illumination. It highlights with considerable poignancy Tom's need for Anna in a matriarchal house he cannot order, and the young Will's predatory control over Anna at this stage in their relationship:

He went on till the illumination fell on him dimly. Then looking up, through the blur, he saw the youth and the girl together, the youth with his back against the wall, his head sunk over the head of the girl. He even saw ... bunches of roosting fowls, up in the night, strange shadows cast from the lantern on the floor. (p. 114)

I say predatory because of the significant posture of Will, but Lawrence says it explicitly and with the same imagery a few pages earlier:

Suddenly, with an incredibly quick, delicate, movement, he put his arms round her and drew her to him. It was quick, cleanly done, like a bird that swoops and sinks close, closer. He was kissing her throat. His eyes were ... like a hawk's. (p. 112)

Will is very much in charge, their marital birth seems quite imminent, and his second carving, not surprisingly, depicts the creation of Eve. Lawrence realizes that the timing of the carving should be appropriate for the reader, because Will ultimately has the message so pathetically wrong. For after he finally overtakes her in the sheaves scene, a pattern of their future struggle is established which is quite similar to that in the preceding generation. The moon has been shining brightly all night, and before examining Will's reaction after the incident with the sheaves, it is important to note that for Lawrence the moon is "the center of our terrestrial individuality in the cosmos. She is the declaration of our existence in separateness" *(Fantasia of the Unconscious,* pp. 191-192). Ursula will respond to this declaration as properly as Will will abrogate his responsibility as a man under it with Anna.

Rhythm, psychology, and unmitigated sexuality rarely will combine more poetically in Lawrence's fiction than during the sheaves scene. I connect only those parts that make the pattern most obvious:

And he had to put up her two sheaves, which had fallen down. He worked in silence. The rhythm of the work carried him away again, as she was coming near. They worked together, coming and going, in a rhythm which carried their feet and their bodies in tune. She stooped, she lifted the burden of sheaves, she turned her face to the dimness where he was, and went with her burden over the stubble. . . . But there was a space between them, and he went away, the work carried them, rhythmic. . . . Into the rhythm of his work there came *a pulse and a steadied purpose.* . . . And the whole rhythm of him beat into his kisses, and still he pursued her. . . . (p. 119, my italics)

Even the phrase "pulse and a steadied purpose" is identical to the one used when Tom and Anna were in the barn – an identity that attests to the basic theory of life rhythm working in both scenes. It does not require much critical ingenuity to recognize here a sustained example of Lawrence's use of the frictional, pulsing to-and-fro which works up to crisis. But the real crisis occurs, as I implied, *after* he overtakes her. The moment is significant for our understanding of Will and the problem of birth. It begins inconspicuously enough: "'Anna' he said in wonder and the birthpain of love." Lawrence grants him the birthpain, for in *Fantasia of the Unconscious* he admits that there is a kind of birth: "In his consummation in the emotional passion of a woman, man is reborn, which is quite true" (pp. 133-134). But Will does not even grant Anna a courteous second for reflection. They conclude their pseudo-intercourse, naturally enough, with a kiss, and Anna happily withdraws to enjoy her happy moment. But note Will's response under the *moon,* the symbol of that separatist ability to be alone: "It hurt him when she drew away from his breast. It hurt him with a chagrin. Why did she draw away from him?" (p. 120). How familiar is the simple language (cf., Lawrence on Tom: "She was not really his. . . . She might go away." [55]), and how frightfully consistent the psychological pattern of the male Brangwens. It is that over-sympathetic male, a victim of his own insecurity, who denies the justifiably separatist response of the female because he predicates his success in life (i.e., his birth) on the foundation of his relationship with the female. In fact, as if Will is mortally hurt by her drawing away, Lawrence finishes him off in no uncertain terms:

> Suddenly he said, as the simple solution stated itself to him:
> "We'll get married, Anna."
> She was silent.
> "We'll get married, Anna, shall we?"
> She stopped in the field again and kissed him, clinging to him passionately, in a way he could not understand. But he left it all now, to marriage. That was the solution now, fixed ahead. He wanted her, he wanted to be married to her, he wanted to have her altogether, as his own for ever.   (pp. 120–121)

The pathetic redundancy of rhythm further reflects the immature state of Will at the time of the proposal: "We'll get married, Anna . . . . We'll get married, Anna, shall we? . . . he could not understand. . . . He wanted her, he wanted to be married to her." It is the childish rhetoric of a minor tantrum.

Lawrence describes in sharp critical terms and with the metaphor of rebirth the man who over-estimates the value of his "reborn of woman" stage. He also forecasts almost exactly the position of Will shortly after the marriage in this passage from *Fantasia of the Unconscious:*

> His consummation is in feeling, not in action. Now, his activity is all of the domestic order and all his thought goes to proving that nothing matters except that birth shall continue and woman shall rock in the nest of the globe like a bird who covers her eggs in some tall tree. Man is the fetcher, the carrier, the sacrifice, the crucified, and the reborn of woman.   (p. 134)

Thus the carving of the creation of Eve by Will is, like the Phoenix, ironically appropriate – for Will has gone to great lengths to prove that man really is reborn of woman. Like Tom Brangwen and like Anton Skrebensky, Will cannot recognize the separatist assertion of his wife because he is unable to function separately or outside her orbit. Anna says yes to Will's proposal, Lydia accepted Tom's, and Ursula will say no to Anton's. Is it at all doubtful that Will would cry like Skrebensky if Anna gave him an outright refusal here? Indeed, there has hardly been any indication of the existence of a purposive self for Will Brangwen throughout his courtship with Anna. He makes carvings and knows his church architecture, but his *raison d'être* does not extend beyond his girlfriend. During a description of a phase in their courting, Lawrence's insistently qualifying "buts" catch that important distinction between Will's dangerous reliance on Anna and Anna's intelligently proportioned appreciation of him: "But for him she was the essence of life. . . . But to him she was a flame that consumed him . . . till he existed only as an unconscious, dark transit of flame, deriving from her" (pp. 125-126). Note that he is "derived" from her – again the Eve carving is debunked – and Anna has the evidence of her own experience to support her when she later argues with him about the appropriateness of both the smallness of the Eve carving, and his belief that Eve came from Adam. Will's carving, as Anna well knows, is the lie of his life.

Lawrence is emphatic in the wedding scene about the "unfinished", "unformed", and "unestablished" (all his adjectives, p. 131) aspects of Anna's stepfather's life. His strategy of focusing on the old marriage just as the new one begins is a way of emphasizing the similar psychologies behind them. What Lawrence bemoans about Tom is not that his life is "unfinished" in the sense that he lacks a comfortable lower middle-class niche; but that because Tom married before he was born he did not have ample opportunity to establish himself as his own man: "He was still as unsure and unfixed as when he had married himself" (p. 131). "Unsure" here means uncertain and "unfixed" means much the same thing – it isn't any existentialist period of voluntary wandering. I think Alan Friedman pushes his brilliant thesis too far when he implies that this kind of lack of fixity may be a strength in a Lawrence character.[10] Tom's condition, unlike Ursula's, is not one of choice, for it is the reflection of his own weaknesses as a human being. When Lawrence writes about Tom and his relation to the cosmos that "there was no end, no finish, only this roaring vast space", we must be careful to disassociate Tom's aimlessness from the glorious awareness of Lawrence's open-ended universe. At Anna's wedding the unformed, semi-born Tom presides over the marriage of his step-daughter to the insecure Will Brangwen. Tom is

[10]   See Friedman, Chapter Six, Part one.

loud, drunk, and naturally oblivious to the psychology that is repeating itself in his family. But the noise begins to lessen, and with music as a background to the softly rhythmic choral arrangement of "listening" and "hearing", Lawrence freezes the chapter in stasis and starts the marriage off on a moment of complete and deceptive silence:

Anna Brangwen had started up, listening, when the music began. She was afraid.
    "It's the wake," he *whispered.*
    She remained tense, her heart beating heavily, possessed with strange, strong fear. Then there came the burst of men's singing, rather uneven. She strained still, *listening.*
    "It's Dad," she said, in a low voice. They were silent, *listening.*
    "And my father," he said.
    She *listened* still. But she was sure. She sank down again into bed, into his arms. He held her very close, kissing her. The hymn rambled on outside, all the men singing their best, having forgotten everything else under the spell of the fiddles and the tune. The firelight glowed against the darkness in the room. Anna could *hear* her father singing with gusto.
    "Aren't they silly," she *whispered.*
    And they crept closer, closer together, hearts beating to one another. *And even as the hymn rolled on, they ceased to hear it.* (p. 139, my italics)

The last line of this passage, quite uncoincidentally, has all the syntactical rhythm of the description in the church when Anna and Will first met. Like the circular pattern of the generations, which repeats itself and "moves out" slightly, the relationship between Anna and Will has begun its circular motion: for when an infatuated Anna heard him that day in church, Lawrence wrote that "still the hymn rolled on, and still she laughed" (p. 106). But now, during the deepening sounds of silence on their wedding night, they both "ceased to hear it" – they are oblivious to the desperate rhythm of the generations which now creates the psychology behind Anna and Will's marriage.

    Lawrence sounds that rhythm as abruptly as possible. The first view of Anna and Will as a married couple focuses directly on the literal and metaphorical aspects of Will's nudity. Will is conventional and very incomplete, and he is described accordingly as a naked child pulled from the womb as he experiences that limited but exciting marriage birth: "Suddenly, like a chestnut falling out of a burr, he was shed naked and glistening on to a soft, fecund earth, leaving behind him the hard rind of worldly knowledge and experience" (p. 141). Nudity, of course, is at the core of marriage as fact and marriage as metaphorical ideal. Lawrence remarks in his letters that it is a man's fundamental need to "love his wife completely and implicitly and in entire nakedness of body and spirit".[11] The collective nakedness of body *and* spirit is what Lawrence demands. And Will soon loses his sexual inhibitions only to reveal to his wife those deeper psychological needs that cannot be satisfied in the passion of a wedding bed. We recall that Lydia Brangwen took sexual initiative with Tom and established a dogmatic pattern which stressed her own separatist inviolability. After Anna tears Will's sexual reticence apart, so does she initiate the return to the purposive life: she unequivocally tells her husband to get out of bed and make contact with the world. But Will's annoyed response is predictable in terms of the psychological syndromes established in the novel. It is always a temptation for Tom and Skrebensky, and even for the more spiritual Will, to predicate their marital rebirth strictly in terms of sex, and thus retreat into the physical drowse of what Lawrence calls "blood intimacy". Their women, all justifiably avowed worshippers of their man's body, worship only to the point of physical satisfaction – never to the adolescent's extreme of delimiting idolatry.

In that same half-illumination and twilight mistiness that now moves from the barn to the bedroom, Anna finds that "the vagueness gave her scope and set her free" (p. 144). "Scope" is a crucial word in the Lawrence lexicon, with its implications about breadth of concern, extent of influence, and "unknowns" to explore. Indeed, "scope" conveniently provides an index to Lawrence's evaluation of how free each character really gets, and thus how close each comes to the suffering of complete rebirth. Will is the same person who panicked in the barn when Anna

[11] *Letters*, p. 280.

drew away from him. He sophomorically feels that complete birth is as close as his marriage bed, and like his uncle before him, he verbalizes his own error in exactly the same terms as Tom: "Indeed, it was true as they said, that a man wasn't born before he was married. What a change indeed" (p. 146). And that is all it should be – *a change*, a preliminary birth along the way to complete rebirth. But Lawrence realizes how frequently man commits the mistake of making this first birth his last. For so often, as Lawrence disappointedly says, "there is the point at which we all now stick" *(Fantasia of the Unconscious, p. 133).* And when Anna rebuffs him because of his sycophantic nagging, Will finds that "never had his soul felt so flayed and uncreated" (p. 148). For Lawrence the term "soul" has two meanings, and context always provides the clue to which is appropriate. It specifically stands for the instinctual self, and, in a general way, it represents the whole essential being of an individual. The latter meaning applies to the quotation above, and it is simply Lawrence's statement that never was it more apparent to Will that his purposive self had not emerged than when he was criticized by his wife. Just as with Tom, Will's awareness of his own incompleteness is translated into periods of bitterness towards the beloved who highlights this deficiency.

Thus the alternating rhythm of hate and love, with its accompanying pulsing language, is very similar to that in the previous generation. For instance, Will fights against his wife's annoyance at him with a total insensitivity to her, and the following results:

Suddenly he saw that she was hurt. He had only seen her triumphant before. Suddenly his heart was torn with compassion for her. (p. 151)

This sort of lightning emotional reversal is identical in sound to the rhetoric of the psychological rebound that Tom experienced in the same situation:

Suddenly, in a flash, he saw she might be lonely, isolated, unsure. She had seemed to him the utterly certain, satisfied, absolute, excluding him. Could she need anything? (p. 89)

Will Brangwen's repeated refusals to permit Anna's right to a separate existence – yes, her right even to ignore him – relates to his insecure, over-sympathetic attachment to her, and it reflects the condition Lawrence explicitly describes in *Psychoanalysis and the Unconscious*: "A soul cannot come into its own through that love alone which is unison. If it stress the one mode, the sympathetic mode, beyond a certain point, it breaks its own integrity, and corruption sets in the living organism" (p. 40). And Will is very corrupt, a veritable predatory demon, as Lawrence describes him:

There followed two black and ghastly days, when she was set in anguish against him, and he felt as if he were in a black, violent underworld, and his wrists quivered murderously. And she resisted him. He seemed a dark, almost evil thing, pursuing her, hanging on to her, burdening her. She would give anything to have him removed. (p. 148)

The reference to "wrists" and "hanging" summarizes the consistent emphasis, even in less volatile situations, on Will's hands throughout the novel. At different times the hands are the symbols ("collective" fixed symbols) of Will's indelicate grasping for control over Anna, or of his significantly overly delicate spirituality, or as the means of polar communication between Anna and Will:

It [the colour] lit on the dark wood of the pew, on the stone, worn aisle, on the pillar behind her cousin, and on her cousin's hands, as they lay on his knees (p. 105). . . . His hovering near her, wanting her to be with him, the futility of him, the way his hands hung, irritated her beyond bearing (p. 148). . . . His hand was curiously sensitive, shrinking, as he shut the door (p. 151). . . . His hands were delicate upon her, and she loved them. But there ran through her the thrill, crisp as pain, for she felt the darkness and other-world still in his soft, sheathed hands (p. 177).

That Will's hands, like Will himself, can be both sensitive and sexually appealing to Anna, and loathesomely grasping and repugnant to her, is evidence of Lawrence's belief in the rhythm of the creative flux – that pattern of polarized adjustment which changes love to hate with the warm speed of an electric vibration.

A major cause of Will's inability to be intimate with Anna without making those pitiful attempts to restrict her freedom (cf. "She fought to keep herself free of him", p. 166) is the diversion of his sympathetic flow. He channels off too much of his emotion to the church. Whatever leftover "energy" he gives to his wife is given with the expectation of final funds invested that must pay dividends. For the church is a wife to Will: "In church he wanted a dark nameless emotion, the emotion of all the great mysteries of passion" (p. 155). In the introduction to *Fantasia of the Unconscious* Lawrence explains "the near relationship between the religious motive and the sexual" (p. 60). Both of these associated motives should be subordinate to a man's sense of passionate, purposive activity. Again, it is not just that Will overestimates the function of the religious motive – we can grant that "all the great mysteries" is too much of a burden for any church – but that outside of his marriage bed or beyond the altar is a world that he will not confront. We recall that when he was "shed naked" after he was married, he was described as "leaving behind him the hard rind of worldly knowledge and experience" (p. 141). But even a romanticist, which Lawrence surely is not, knows that you can never leave all that behind. Perhaps it is proper to ask why a man should alter the happy, diurnal rhythm of afternoon church and evening sex. Those who accuse Lawrence either of Puritanism or libertinism will be pleased by the eminently balanced tone of his response: "You have got to keep your sexual fulfilment even then subordinate, just subordinate to the great passion of purpose: subordinate by a hair's breadth only: but still, by that hair's breadth, subordinate" *(Fantasia of the Unconscious,* p. 145). By "sexual" here Lawrence also includes the "religious" – that is, he means any passionate fulfillment that does not *directly* contribute to a man's sense of personal achievement. It is one of the ironies and successes of Will Brangwen's life that eventually he translates his sexual-religious fervor into purposive activity by working constructively in the church. Yet before he obtains his teaching position, he must fight the vicious, complicated battle for birth outlined in "Anna Victrix".

The "Anna Victrix" chapter provides the most sustained exam-

ple of what Lawrence means by his rhythmic stylistic use of modified repetition, a repetition justified by his belief "that every
natural crisis in emotion or passion or understanding comes
from this pulsing, frictional to-and-fro which works up to culmination". If we can separate these terms momentarily, there
are crises of passion in this chapter, which primarily concern
the role of sex; crises of emotion, which involve such episodes
as Will's placement of his tools; and crises of understanding that
emphasize Will and Anna's different conceptions of the church.
These distinctions, of course, are schematic and artificial, because a crisis in understanding about the church, for instance,
reflects the emotional commitments that Will has which soon
lead to pseudo-passionate extremes. But the central rhythm of
their marriage is unmistakeable:

So it went on continually, the recurrence of love and conflict between them. One day, it seemed as if everything was shattered, all
life spoiled, ruined, desolate and laid waste. The next day it was all
marvelous again, just marvelous. One day she thought she would
go mad from his very presence, the sound of his drinking was
detestable to her. The next day she loved and rejoiced in the way he
crossed the floor, he was sun, moon and stars in one.   (p. 164)

This lack of stability takes its exhausting toll on Anna; Lawrence
describes how she feels when Will leaves the house, by return-
ing significantly to the metaphors of flow and the quest for freedom: "Then the flow of her life, which he seemed to damn up, was
let loose, and she was free. She was free, she was full of delight"
(p. 164). The pattern of the female's excitement at her parasitic
male's departure is the same as experienced by Lydia; and like
her mother, Anna is described "as a flower that has been tempted forth into blossom" (p. 166), and "like a flower in the
sun" (p. 167). As in the last generation, this procreative potential becomes stifled by the deadening influence of her man's
insecurity.

However, passages like the following appear to indicate that
the stillborn state of their marriage is Anna's fault as much as
Will's: "He felt, somewhere, that she did not respect him. She
only respected him as far as he was related to herself" (p.

167). Will's point is well-taken, but it does not go back to first causes. We must not forget that Anna's lack of respect for Will – which develops after their marriage – has its origin in his preying and sychophantic attacks upon her. As I implied previously, she also reacts to Will's religiosity by over-compensating in her own attitudes toward the church. That is, we recall that as a young girl, Anna rejected the church because she found unpalatable its formalized body of knowledge and its mystical experiences inadequately formulated in empty language. Yet after they are married she is enraged further because Will not only admires the church, but he seems to love it as a substitute for purposive human activity – and nearly a substitute for the sexual experience itself. Revolted by the position of her husband, Anna makes her own error as she derides Will's belief in the church in the most anti-Lawrentian terms possible; she asserts the primacy of the mind and of knowledge over blood consciousness and mystical apprehension: "Did he believe the water turned to wine at Cana? She would drive him to the thing as a historical fact: so much rain-water – look at it – can it become grape-juice, wine? . . . It was true for him. His mind was extinguished at once, his blood was up" (p. 168). In short, Will Brangwen's excessive reliance on the church has driven Anna from the mystical appreciation of church doctrine that Lawrence applauds to the rationalist skepticism he abhors: "She, almost against herself, clung to the worship of the human knowledge. . . . She believed in the omnipotence of the human mind" (p. 169). "Almost against herself" – the phrase rings out poignantly after Anna's mature objections to the church which she had as an adolescent.

Lawrence describes some of the ruling principles of his vision of life with some interesting metaphors in a passage from *Fantasia of the Unconscious,* and the description also summarizes the essence of the church-knowledge conflict between Anna and Will:

There is continual conflict between the soul, which is forever sending forth incalculable impulses, and the psyche, which is conservative, and wishes to persist in its old motions, and the mind, which wishes to have "freedom," that is, spasmodic, idea-driven control. . . . We must live by all three, ideal, impulse, and tradition, each in its hours. (pp. 165–166)

It is the responsibility of each person to balance the ideal of the mind, the impulses of the soul, and the tradition of the psyche – Lawrence's voluntaristic version, it seems to me, of the id, ego, and super-ego, respectively. But whether restructured Freudian dogma or not, these psychological distinctions are at the very core of the rhythmic struggle between Anna and Will. Their battles are indicative of the stress that they alternately place on different modes of living. Thus form and content become so properly hard to separate in this novel because the description of the rhythm of their life style (i.e., syntax, metaphor, and incident) always reflects the psychology of the particular situation. The birth to freedom metaphor, of course, is the most obvious use of rhythm. For instance, Anna absorbs herself in pregnancy, and despite Will's need for the church, which frequently excludes her, she finds that briefly "she was complete in herself" (p. 176) – a pun of large proportions. And expectedly "he was ashamed that he could not come to fulfillment without her" (p. 179). Anna's feeling of freedom is shortlived, a testament to the fact that pregnancy is an inadequate basis for the organic completeness she desires. Although she occasionally had "rebirths of old exaltation" (p. 179), there can be no meaningful birth for her with Will as an incubus: "For her there was no final release, since he could not be liberated from himself" (p. 179). The echo of Tom Brangwen – "and still he could not get free" – sounds mournfully clear.

It is a critical stage in Anna's life. Filled with the joys of pregnancy, near a temporarily stabilizing kind of completeness, she requires only a resolution of her conflict with Will to have experienced her own (not merely give) birth. But no understanding is reached. What cannot be resolved through any fundamental compromise is concluded by Anna herself by symbolically exerting her own power. For Anna finds she has "no one to exult with" – her husband exults with his church – so she "danced before the unknown" (p. 179).[12] Every being in Lawrence's universe, whether male or female, animal or plant, must sustain itself by communication with a life force which never can be fully apprehended. In a "balanced" marriage the relatively equal depths of the unknowable unconscious (the unconscious which is, "by its very nature, unanalyzable, undefinable, inconceivable [*Psychoanalysis and the Unconscious*, p. 15]) in each partner serves as the channel through which this necessary urge to reach the unknown is directed. As intimacy develops between two lovers, so will a corresponding awareness of each other's unknowable life force affirm the health of their union. This idea is not simply a more elaborate version of familiarity breeding contempt, and neither is it a sophomoric notion of absurdly mystical implications. It is really quite conventional if we translate its basic psychology into the framework of Lawrence's stress on the sustaining value of "separateness" in any heterosexual relationship. To commune with the unknown is to retreat into that solitude which belongs to one lover and not the other – that is, which recognizes and grants some inviolable "otherness" that will tolerate no intrusion by a mate. A blatantly symbolic thrust for the unknown becomes unnecessary when a person can experience those depths merely by communicating with his husband, wife, or lover. The symbolic maneuvers seem like justifiable mystical masturbation brought on by the lack of a deep and rewarding relationship with another person. Thus in a Lawrentian marriage, Birkin will stop throwing stones, Anna will not need to dance, and Ursula will not have to commit her excusable murder under the moon: They will get their stimulation elsewhere.

But Anna Brangwen dances to "annul" Will Brangwen (p. 180), and the verb is perfectly chosen by Lawrence: she wipes him and the marriage off the records, for with his obsequious need for his wife, his lust for the church, and his lack of satis-

---

[12]   Lawrence discusses this "unknown" in his letters: "Love is, that I go to a woman to know myself, and knowing myself, to go further, to explore in to the unknown, which is the woman, venture in upon the coasts of the unknown, and open my discovery to all humanity." *Letters*, p. 318.

fying depth, Will has not really consummated his marital responsibility. He leaves a frustrated wife, for he is impotent and
annulment proceedings are in order. In an interesting short essay Lawrence wrote late in his life, he describes a woman dancing in terms that recall Yeats's description at the end of "Among
School Children":

To the music one should dance, and dancing, dance. The estrucan
young woman is going gaily at it, after two thousand five hundred
years. She is not making love to music, nor is the dark limbed youth,
her partner. She is just dancing her very soul into existence, having
made an offering to the lively phallus of man, on the other hand, to
the shut womb symbol. So she is quite serene, and dancing herself
as a very fountain of life.[13]

Although Yeats's reconciling "unity of being" idea is reached for
in this dance, the pathos of its absence as an achievement by
Anna is quite evident. For Anna has made both the offers referred to in this passage, but Will drives her into the "shut womb
symbol" as her only means of expression with the unknown.
Will's phallus cannot stand erect without a church altar or Anna
to prop it up – and by "lively phallus", of course, Lawrence
has more in mind for the male than sexual intercourse. It is a
metaphor for the male as functioning, purposeful, "alive" animal. Lawrence holds his males' maleness (not masculinity) to
very strict account; Will has not paid his due, he must be nulli-
fied. Or if we can picture a lonely Anna despairing of her mate,
and orchestrating by default her own dance to her own tune before her own version of the unknown (whom can she dance
with?), Lawrence's concluding metaphor in this passage from
Fantasia of the Unconscious is very relevant:

Once man vacates his camp of sincere, passionate positivity in dis-
interested being, his supreme responsibility to fulfil his own pro-
foundest impulses, with reference to none but God or his own soul,
not taking woman into count at all, in this primary responsibility to
his own deepest soul; once man vacates this strong citadel of his own
genuine not spurious divinity, then in comes woman, picks up the
sceptre, and begins to conduct a rag-time band.   (p. 135)

[13] D. H. Lawrence, "Making Love to Music", 1928, in *Sex, Literature, and
Censorship* (New York, 1959), p. 45.

A camp and citadel have been vacated, and Anna now will dance to her own band.

In what Lawrence calls "the blackness of the shadow" (p. 180), Will Brangwen watches Anna dance. No doubt he is barely visible as man or husband, just as the obliterated Tom looked like a vague ghost as he watched his pregnant wife lie in the darkness. These two key scenes, with their similar use of light and theme, show a measure of the different life attitudes of the two women in their contrasting postures while pregnant in the semidarkness before their observing husbands. Both are formidable, "separatist" women, and although Lydia is weak on a bed because of her advanced pregnancy, Lydia could never exert her power as Anna does in this scene even if she were in her first month. Both men are about equally emasculated. As Anna dances, the rhythm of Lawrence's emotional, "fourth-dimensional" prose, with its characteristic repetitive phraseology (i.e., "danced", "exulting") is structured around another pulsing toward crisis; three sentences, each double the length of the previous one, increase the tempo and work up to Anna's mystical, masturbatory climax:

And she had to dance in exultation beyond him. Because he was in the house, she had to dance before her Creator in exemption from the man. On a Saturday afternoon, when she had a fire in the bedroom, again she took off her things and danced, lifting her knees and her hands in a slow, rhythmic exulting.   (p. 180)

And a moment later Lawrence repeats the process, with a syntactical repetitive insistence that sways hypnotically with Anna's motions:

He stood near the door in the blackness of shadow, watching transfixed. And with slow, heavy movements, she swayed backwards and forwards, like a full ear of corn, pale in the dusky afternoon, threading before the firelight, dancing his non-existence, dancing herself to the Lord, to exultation.   (p. 181)

Throughout all this Will is described as "burned alive" as though he "were at the stake", much in the manner that Skrebensky first senses his nullification, uncoincidentally I would suppose, at Joan of Arc's city of Rouen. The familiar birth metaphor of escape and the "rainbow-foundation" symbol then combine in convenient terms:

And the shame was a bitter fire in him, that she was everything to him, that he had nothing but her. And then she would taunt him with it, that he could not escape. The fire went black in his veins. For try as he might, he could not escape. She was everything to him, she was his life and his derivation. He depended on her. If she were taken away, he would collapse as a house *from which the central pillar is removed.*   (p. 183, my italics)

The echo of Tom's situation is quite evident: "He felt like a broken arch thrust sickeningly out for support" (p. 60). And Lawrence summarizes the relevance of these clipped rainbow symbols in *Fantasia of the Unconscious* when he insists that "the life circuit of living creatures is built upon the arch which spans the duality of living beings" (p. 189). This arch really will not be seen until the last page of the novel. It consists, among other elements, of the separatist and sympathetic pillars of support – and Will lacks the former. Occasionally Anna takes him back, and "sometimes for a moment she had pity". But Lawrence wisely considers this ultimately condescending female attitude quite damaging to a marriage. When man too emphatically gives up his male role as purposive being, the female "keeps pity and tenderness emblazoned on her banners. But God help the man who she pities. Ultimately she tears him to bits" (*Fantasia of the Unconscious,* p. 134). Lawrence is saying that there are more subtle yet equally potent ways to take apart the emasculated male than to destroy his already damaged being under a blazing moon. As Anna nears the birth light, so will Will feel these subtleties with meaningful pain.

But every marriage adjusts with changing time and circumstance, and a temporary resolution of their marital conflict is expressed through that traditional metaphor of drowning. For many months Will has been described as sinking into deep water, unable to stand by himself: "Why was she the all, the everything, why must he sink if he were detached from her (p. 183). . . . Can a man tread the unstable water all his life, and call that

standing (p. 184) . . . . She might push him off into the deeps"
(p. 184). What is implicit in all this water imagery is that old
process of drowning leading to rebirth: Will *must* go in deep water by himself – that is, without Anna; he must drown himself
in the waters of the world, of society, to encourage his birth as
a secure and independent man. After he is born, Will's uncle Tom
literally will drown, but Will's submerging is far more pleasant:
"A vagueness had come over everything, like a drowning. And
it was an infinite relief to drown, a relief, a great, great relief. . . .
He would force her no more" (p. 186). Will's decision here to
"give in" simply is based on his exhaustion from his struggles
with his wife. Thus at this stage in his life Will still has no independent, purposive being. Yet although he still depends on his
wife, he finally does grant her a measure of separateness, and
Lawrence appropriately defines this stage in Will's life as a qualified rebirth: 'He had come into his own existence. He was born
for a second time, born at last into himself, out of the vast body
of humanity" (p. 187). We know the birth is not nearly complete because of the obvious absence of a purposive self in him.
He still "felt that the whole of the man's world was exterior and
extraneous to his own real life with Anna" (p. 190). Anna, however, does have the potential to strive for "the infinite and unknown" without predicating her success in this quest only on the
basis of her relationship with her mate. She is strong enough to
ask herself if she should travel beyond maternity and domesticity, and the questions naturally call forth the expanding symbol
of the novel:

And from her Pisgah mount, which she had attained, what could she
see? A faint, gleaming horizon, a long way off, and a rainbow like
an archway, a shadow-door with faintly coloured coping above it.
Must she be moving thither? . . . Dawn and sunset were the feet of
the rainbow that spanned the day, and she was the hope, the promise.
Why should she travel any further?   (p. 192)

So Anna sees the rainbow – significantly faintly and from a distance – while her mother never even glimpsed it. After she
approaches the symbol with the rhetoric of cautious questioning, she rejects it. It is "the hope", "the promise", but never the

realizable fact for her, and she gives up the battle for the most conventional of reasons:

There was another child coming, and Anna lapsed into vague content. If she were not the wayfarer to the unknown, if she were arrived now, settled in her builded house, a rich woman, still her doors opened under the arch of the rainbow. (p. 193)

She abandons the quest in favor of the comforts of a room with a view.

But the struggle for birth continues. There is one more intense battle in the "escape to freedom" motif that must be fought before Will Brangwen can express his purposive self, before Will cannot only be alone but also chart a constructive path out of his solitude. It concerns that fundamental disagreement between him and his wife about Will's over-emphasis on the church. The emasculated Will Brangwen, with his carvings, paintings, architectural idolatry, and later with his attempted seduction, virtually has been masturbating for a hundred pages, until "here in the church. . . . Brangwen came to his consummation" (p. 199). The Hopkins-like rhythm of the soul's transport is unmistakeable here, with the crucial thematic difference that the rhythm reflects Will's *substitution* of the spiritual orgasm for meaningful sexual communion with his wife:

Here the stone leapt up from the plain of earth, leapt up in a manifold, clustered desire each time, up, away from the horizontal earth, through twilight and dusk and the whole range of desire, through the swerving, the declination, ah, to the ecstasy, the touch, to the meeting and the consummation, the meeting, the clasp, the close embrace, the neutrality, the perfect, swooning consummation, the timeless ecstasy. There his soul remained, at the apex of the arch, clinched in the timeless ecstasy, consummated. (p. 199)

Hopkins' rhythm is simulated – "the declination, ah, to the ecstasy, the touch" – for this quasi-sexual passage, with its necessary elimination of explicit transition, is Lawrence's extreme version of his use of repetition (cf., "meeting", "ecstasy") to build rhythmically to a climactic moment of passion. Since we have no evidence that Lawrence saw the echoing "Windhover" poem before it was published in 1918, the thematic content of this passage is coincidentally quite provocative. Will is a sort of windhover *manqué*, for his etherialized habits and his lack of an imposing presence make Lawrence describe him consistently as a "bird" who always "hovers". And indeed, he metaphorically leaves the ground again in one repetitive sentence in the cavernous church:

Then again he gathered himself together, in transit, every jet of him strained and leaped, leaped clear into the darkness above, to the fecundity and the unique mystery, to the touch, the clasp, the consummation, the climax of eternity, the apex of the arch. (p. 199)

A very picturesque leap, no doubt − but not nearly far enough to reach "the climax of eternity". One does not merely jump for that in a spacious church.

Like Hopkins' poetry, the rhythm of Lawrence's prose when it describes the most intense moments of physical and spiritual consummation tends to be impatient with the ability of conventional transition phrases to convey a particularly ecstatic feeling. Lawrence's prose races breathlessly in a long sentence to the top of the arch with Will, just as the rhythm of Hopkins' poetry omits all connectives as it attempts to keep pace with the soaring bird. We have seen this repetitive prose work in an opposite direction in *The Rainbow*, as Lawrence descends with Will to the bottom of the ocean when Will drowned:

If he relaxed his will would fall, fall through endless space, into the bottomless pit, always falling, will-less, helpless, non-existent, just dropping to extinction, falling till the fire of friction had burned out, like a falling star, then nothing, nothing, complete nothing.
(p. 185)

The similarity between Lawrence's and Hopkins' use of rhythm can be explored one step further before we return to Will and Anna. There is nearly an identical emphasis in Lawrence's and Hopkins' description of design in art. They both justify unconventional rhythm by their belief in an uncompromising adherence to a "fourth dimension", to the melody of "air" − in short, to the very feel of the thing that cannot be felt through ordinary rhythm and cannot be communicated without a dogmatic *sensual* sincerity. Hopkins writes to Bridges:

No doubt – my poetry errs on the side of oddness . . . but as air, melody, is what strikes me most of all in music and design in painting, so *design,* pattern, or what I am in the habit of calling "inscape" is what I above all aim at in poetry.[14]   (my italics)

And Lawrence takes that term "design" and applies it in similar manner to fiction in a passage I alluded to previously:

Design in art is a recognition of the relation between various things, various elements in the creative flux. You can't *invent* a design. You recognize it, in the *fourth dimension.* That is, with your blood and your bones, as well as with your eyes.[15]

Thus when Lawrence describes Will's flight to the ceiling or the sea-bottom, or when Hopkins describes the windhover's journey, both writers reflect what Lawrence calls in his *Study of Thomas Hardy* "the pure will to motion" in life. But not all of Lawrence's prose – certainly a relatively small amount – will contain a pulsing beat that leads to climax. For when a character is not involved in the will to motion, Lawrence comments further: "The very adherence to rhyme and regular rhythm is a concession . . . an admission of the living, positive inertia which is the other half of life, other than the pure will to motion."[16] The terms "living" and "positive" are important: they are firm indications that Lawrence realizes that where there is no motion there is not necessarily boredom, and where there is inertia there need not be stasis. He makes no claim for perpetual ecstasy.

   Both ideas of a "will to motion" and "living inertia" conveniently fit, it seems to me, into Alan Friedman's intelligent belief that Lawrence's technique is an attempt to "render his character's unconscious". In scenes that have unconventional rhythm and a kind of hyperbolic rhetoric (e.g., the drowning, cathedral, sexual scenes, etc.), Friedman explains that Lawrence "is attempting to render the fluid, nonconscious, or dark mental processes, while at the same time remaining wholly within the region of con-

---

[14]   C. C. Abbott, ed., *The Letters of Gerard Manley Hopkins to Robert Bridges* (London, 1935), p. 66.
[15]   "Art and Morality", in *Phoenix,* p. 525.
[16]   "Study of Thomas Hardy", in *Phoenix,* p. 478.

ventional and conscious syntax".[17] He means "conventional" only insofar as the syntax does not throw out *all* explicit transition (as in Molly Bloom's soliloquy), and consequently he uses "conscious" because the syntax is offered above the level of stream of consciousness. Friedman notes in his analysis of passages like Anna's dance of annihilation that it is understandably impossible for Lawrence or the reader to find objective correlatives for phrases like "he felt he was being burned alive". Thus Friedman really says what Lawrence maintains about the rhythm of life and art: the rhythm of Lawrence's art is based on the psychology of life; and because certain psychological patterns can more fully be "felt" than devoured by exegesis, the rhythm of the description and/or the use of adjectives by Lawrence often defy conventional analysis and beg for that "fourth-dimensional" appreciation by the "blood and bones", as Lawrence calls it, of a sensitive reader. Friedman's phrase "stream of the unconscious" is appropriate, and his belief that this "unconscious" ultimately is not open to explicit paraphrase is borne out by Lawrence's statement that the unconscious is "by its very nature, unanalyzable, undefinable, inconceivable" *(Psychoanalysis and the Unconscious,* p. 15). Because the unconscious cannot be paraphrased, and because the psychology of Lawrence's art concerns the unconscious, the best approach to Lawrence's fiction may be the one that attempts to isolate this necessarily elusive psychology by focusing on associated patterns of rhythm. By working with rhythm and doctrine in this way it is easier to understand the minimal knowledge that Lawrence does feel we have about the unconscious (cf. *Psychoanalysis and the Unconscious* and *Fantasia of the Unconscious),* and to see how this knowledge is displayed in the characteristic rhythms of the novel.

The movement from the cathedral scene to the emergence of the final, qualified birth of Anna and Will is a short but bitterly contested step. With the sad lessons of other Brangwens behind her, Anna knows "what the roof of the church left out" and "she claimed the right to freedom above her, higher than the

[17]   Friedman, pp. 164-165.

roof. She had always a sense of being roofed in" (p. 200). It is precisely that absolutist flight of Will's to the ceiling which Lawrence criticizes here. The best way Anna can exert this claim, since she already has given up about reaching the "unknown", is to spoil with justified bitterness Will's unfortunate sublimated "passionate intercourse" with the cathedral. It is *not* that the passion is inappropriate, but as an absolute, an ideal end-point of ecstasy, it is inadequate and onanistic. Thus Anna regards the idealized status of the church with unqualified disgust; she realizes the kind of sexual distortion which Will's spiritual masturbation implies, so she unmercifully berates her star-struck husband about the question of the sexual identity of the statues. The wickedly smiling statues are blind neo-Victorian relics of the discrepancy between the word, and the word made flesh; between what Will thinks he should feel as a "religious man" and what his phallus tells him he feels: "They winked and leered, giving suggestion of the many things that had been left out of the great concept of the church" (p. 201). Will argues that they are men, Anna that they are women – but Lawrence's point (and, no doubt, Anna's also) is that the castrated, soul-centered statues make sexual identification tragically irrelevant. The statues reflect Will's own sexual confusions and serve as symbolic summaries of Anna's complaint. Her polemics prove cumulatively effective, and with his absolutist belief in the church damaged, Will significantly reacts for the first time – there has not been *any previous reference* of this sort – to the sensual fullness, freedom, and fertility of nature. He has been cleansed and enlightened:

He listened to the thrushes in the gardens and heard a note which the cathedrals did not include: something free and careless and joyous. He crossed a field that was all yellow with dandelions, on his way to work, and the bath of yellow glowing was something at once so sumptuous and so fresh, that he was glad he was away from his shadowy cathedral. There was life outside the church. (p. 203)

I am reminded of the strikingly similar apocalyptic moment, and almost identical symbolic use of sensuous yellows and blowing fields, in Fitzgerald's short story, "Absolution". In that story,

after Rudolph finally resolves – with Father Schwartz's macabre urging – his own religious confusion, we immediately read
that "outside the window the blue sirocco trembled over the
wheat, and girls with yellow hair walked sensuously along roads
that bounded the fields. . . ."[18] Will has noticed the women, but
never until now the fields.

And Will still cannot quite feel "free" of his own woman because he still introverts the sexual act. His ties to his wife (i.e.,
the tie to himself) still emasculate him, and he attempts to seduce a susceptible girl. Lawrence describes this overflow syndrome with great detail in *Fantasia of the Unconscious:*

> The great resolution of aloneness and appeasedness, and the further
> deep assumption of responsibility in purpose – this is necessary to
> every parent, every father, every husband, at a certain point. If the
> resolution is never made, the responsibility never embraced, then the
> love-making will run on into frenzy, and lay waste to the family.
> (p. 157)

And lay waste it nearly does, until Anna challenges Will to a ca-
thartic phallic hunting-out, a sensual duel of discovery that she
realizes is essential after Will returns from his "frenzy" of attempted seduction in Nottingham. With this adjustment completed, Will sets his house in order, begins to develop the "responsibility of purpose" in a constructive vocation. Thus the
freedom metaphor asserts itself for the last time in relation to
Will: "And gradually, Brangwen began to find himself free to attend to the outside life as well. His intimate life was so violently
active that it set *another man in him free*" (p. 235, my italics).
It is the third and final birth for the second generation Brangwen
in the novel – the birth of a purposive self that follows the
birth of marriage and the birth signified by the destruction of
the cathedral symbol. By her own choice, as I indicated earlier,
Anna glimpses the rainbow but vitiates the potential of complete
organic birth in the lazy daze of giving birth: "She was willing
now to postpone all adventures into unknown realities" (p.
203). Her postponement is eternal, and her daughter picks up

---

[18] The reference to Will Brangwen also recalls the tempting goldenrod,
girls' hair, and seashore images that attract the ascetic in Eliot's "Ash Wed-
nesday".

the rain-check. As the labor pains for the rhythmic struggle for post-natal birth increase, Ursula will inherit the pain and wage the longest fight of all.

3. THE METAPHOR DELIVERED: THE SUNDERING BIRTH OF URSULA

A strained calm reigns at the very center of *The Rainbow,* as the rush of the Marsh flood really sweeps away more than Tom Brangwen. The ceremonious pause after the grandfather's death comes conspicuously just before Lawrence thrusts the third generation Ursula Brangwen into the first of two chapters entitled "The Widening Circle". It is the deceptive stasis before Ursula begins her long passionate struggle for birth. Every chapter now noticeably contributes to the widening, the expanding of this "pregnant" circle, until the full glory of the rainbow arch is experienced by Ursula at the conclusion of the novel. Thus the roaring flood does not purge the novel of the past – the inherited generational rhythms cannot be forgotten; but it does isolate Ursula on the forward crest of its waves as it picks up the momentum of the psychology of the rhythm of birth initiated by Ursula's "separation" from her father in the previous chapter. As a young Ursula Brangwen stands with her grandmother at the end of the flood chapter, and also on the threshold of the unknown future of "The Widening Circle" chapter, Lawrence writes with purposeful deception: "Here was peace and security" (p. 258). But he knows, and Ursula will learn, that it is the peace of stasis, and the specious security of the sentimental backward look. Although the past is awesome – "the greater space" – the future is equally vast and more *unknown.* In the past there is death, domesticity, and compromise, while in the future may be birth.

The long section of *The Rainbow* that involves Ursula is both a summary of psychological patterns isolated earlier in the novel,

and the longest sustained struggle by one person for organic
birth since Anna's relatively compressed version in "Anna Victrix". This second half of the novel recapitulates the problems
that have plagued two generations of Brangwens. It contains a
kind of relentlessness of purpose, a numbing rhythm of battle,
victory, and defeat that continues with little interruption once
the flood recedes. All the problems that we have encountered
earlier, problems about parent-child relationships, sexual adjustment, "purposive being", and religion are treated not only
more extensively, but also more explicitly within the rhythmic
drive for birth. This sprawling section of *The Rainbow* is so steadfast in its direction – as though Lawrence is confident that the
rhythm of two generations has prepared us for this finale –
that it is a kind of *bildungsroman* for organic birth, with the embryo of Ursula always the developing center of attention. Yet the
rhythm of the education process, unlike, for instance, Joyce's
A Portrait of the Artist as a Young Man, builds very little on momentum: it repeatedly drags Ursula through one experience and
into the next without granting her the accumulated capital of a
previous triumph or abnegation to use in her next challenge. For
quite frequently there is no capital to grant. That is, Ursula's increasing power, most realistically, is not cumulative in the conventional sense that it becomes part of an unstoppable glide toward birth. She experiences *at any time* – and even right at
the end – emphatic defeats and she makes frightfully wrong
decisions. Her previous experiences count towards her final
birth, quite simply, because they are the explicit hurdles which
she must overcome to progress further. And she does not really pick up speed along her ontogenetic way because of apocalyptic moments or fine victories; every hurdle must be crossed
as it comes, and they get higher as she gets older (i.e., more
developed). In *The Rainbow* experience does not provide the ability to overcome the next hazard, but the opportunity to be con-
fronted with it in the first place. Ursula must fight her battle as
a school teacher after she struggles with her parents, but her
break with her parents does not make her job at school any
easier. The rhythmic sound of the continuing struggle is not of

increasing tempo but of increasing volume, as each conflict brings Ursula closer to the rainbow and heightens the drama of her impending birth. This rhythm is quite appropriate as a reflection of the psychology of Lawrence's own life, which had periods of chronic depression and extended elation, long stretches of physical discomfort and shorter ones of health – but never that unbelievable momentum that could feed on itself and assure success. Ursula's struggle, therefore, is free from the intrusion of a *deus ex machina* and the benefit of some smaller victory that guarantees the larger one of "birth". The rhythm of her section of the novel is as percussive as Lawrence envisioned life to be. Though Lawrence is aware of the glory of this continuous confrontation, so is he sensitive to the pain it creates and the exhaustion it involves. No doubt many readers lie against that tree with Ursula at the end of the novel. They have traveled the distance between mechanical life and organic birth with her.

*

Ursula's individual victories take the form of "sunderings", as she wrenches herself from delimiting ties with her family, friends, lovers, and religion. It is a gradual process of birth by separation; and "separate" – as verb and adjective – is the recurrent term that Lawrence uses to describe how the psychology of the rhythm of sundering leads to complete "detachment" and birth. This evolution of sundering was not felt in the earlier generations because only Ursula is given the time to separate: she is the only Brangwen woman who makes her mistakes *before* marriage, and thus her unmarried state provides her with greater flexibility to rectify error and separate herself from devitalizing influences. Lawence sounds the psychology of the rhythm of sundering as abruptly as possible. Will paces back and forth, concerned over the fate of his child. "It lay naked and vulnerable at every point", for it has just been born. "It had a separate being", (p. 209) and it is Ursula's long-range objective to grow up *really naked* – or bereft of all hindrances to her undeniable separateness as an organic being. As in the earlier generation, the confrontations between Will and the young Ursula are stressed because an emasculated father has usurped the role of the mother. Increasingly alienated from the affections of his wife, the unconfident Will, who as yet has no purpose in the man's world, has turned both to an idealized love of religion and an unhealthy over-dependence on his daughter, Ursula. He covets the child as he craves the cathedral, and as he nearly smothers the one with excessive, unhealthy love, so does he almost impale his manhood on the other with his intense, overcompensating drive for spiritual sustenance. Ursula's first sundering will be the severance of this birth-retarding umbilical attachment to her father.

That same general psychological pattern which skirts "dynamic spiritual incest" asserts itself between Will and Ursula as it did between Tom and Anna. As Anna, like Lydia, becomes absorbed in domesticity, "Ursula became the child of her father's heart" (p. 210). And like his uncle before him, he unfastened her clothes and "she loved him that he compelled her with his strength and decision" (p. 212). This excitement, of course, is from only a child's perspective, for it is precisely the indecisiveness and insecurity in Will that Anna finds so disturbing. As Will continues to absorb his daughter, Lawrence writes that "she was wakened too soon" (p. 218) – which is exactly the danger of "early arousal" that he fears in *Fantasia of the Unconscious*. In *Psychoanalysis and the Unconscious* and *Fantasia of the Unconscious* the crucial parent-child relationship frequently is described in terms of electricity – in addition to the earlier essay's basic metaphor of the developing embryo's struggle to be born:

The argument is that between an individual and *any* external object with which he has an affective connection there exists a definite vital flow, as definite and concrete as the electric current whose polarized circuit sets our tramcars running and our lamps shining, or our Marconi wires vibrating. Whether this object be human, or animal, or plant, or quite inanimate, there is still a circuit.

(Fantasia of the Unconscious, p. 63)

But the circuit may be interrupted. Indeed, as a central metaphorical and psychological principle Lawrence states that "the electricity of the universe is a sundering force" *(Psychoanalysis and the Unconscious,* p. 22) – and so often Ursula's break from a restriction is described as "electrical flash" or "burning away." In terms of the parent-child relationship, it is always characterized in his essays as a stop-and-go flow of mutual awareness from parent to child: "It is like a lovely, suave, fluid *creative* electricity that flows in a circuit between the great nerve centers" (*Psychoanalysis and the Unconscious,* p. 22). The electrical exchanges between Will and Ursula involve static and awkwardness – they are never described as "creative" for they do not contribute to her birth. Lawrence does not make an obvious error here. He realizes that the path of parental (or sexual) love should not and will not run smoothly. The rhythm of the proper interrelationship must be abrasive enough to guarantee the separate life of the participants: inherent in the parent-child connection, for instance, is the potential – fortunately for Ursula – of the child's necessary, sporadic, and ultimately total alienation.

Despite these suggestions of a quasi-incest that is similar to the previous generation's father-daughter relationship, courage is required in any evaluation of Ursula's total circuit-breaking step away from her father: courage in young Ursula to forget his strong, comforting forearms and break away, courage in the father to comprehend and accept the impending separation (and Will fails here), and courage for many readers to accept the split at Ursula's young age. For frequently the spark of vitality flows electrically between Ursula and Will on what seems a perfectly smooth, well-coordinated circuit. But this deceptive fluidity is simply a manifestation of the ease of Will's adoption of Ursula as a spiritual child-lover, and of Ursula's premature and over-sexual awareness of her father. Placed next to the description of Will and Anna as "in a darkness, passionate, electric" (p. 213), the following similar description about Ursula indicates that Will really has two lovers and is over-dependent on two people:

It had a separate being, but it was his own child. His flesh and blood vibrated to it (p. 209). . . . She was a piece of light that really belonged to him, that played within his darkness. . . . He wanted to live unthinking, with her presence flickering upon him.... From when she was a tiny child Ursula could remember his forearm, with its fine black hairs and its electric flexibility (p. 214)....

"It had a separate being, but" – there can be no buts, as the daughter now begins to make clear.

The electrical impulses between Ursula and Will soon obviously prevent the birth of Ursula. The rhythm of the description of their relationship ceases to be fluid even in the limited manner illustrated above – of a dangerous meeting handled with care and feeling. The prose now becomes clipped and blunt. Will is brutally insensitive to Ursula's needs, for she is merely the depository of his own. As Lawrence expands his metaphor and compresses his prose, Will gives the defenseless Ursula "occasional cruel shocks" (p. 215). In *Psychoanalysis and the Unconscious* Lawrence anticipates the cleavage that shortly occurs in *The Rainbow;* he also summarizes in one passage the justification for many of the painful sunderings that Ursula will undergo to be born:

Life cannot progress without these ruptures, severances, cataclysms; pain is a living reality, not merely a deathly. Why haven't we the courage for life pains? If we could depart from our old tenets of the mind, if we could fathom our own unconscious sapience, we should find we have courage and to spare. We are too mentally domesticated. (p. 21)[1]

"Life cannot progress" – the alternative is not death, but the benumbing stasis exemplified by at least two generations of Brangwen men and women. To use Lawrence's terms, in order to "rupture" a connection, "sever" an affiliation, or feel the painful "cataclysmic" result of the loud and final *noli me tangere*, there must be a felt need for separation, and an emphatic act upon this need. Silence, exile – perhaps – but *no cunning,* for the need for separation is felt not in the brain, but unpremeditatedly, in what Lawrence calls "the blood and the bones" of unconscious intuition. In the Ursula section of *The Rainbow,* the frequency of the term "separate" creates, in Brown's

---

[1] When Anna experienced birthpains, Lawrence praised her with the same language: "It was bad enough. But to her it was never deathly. Even the fierce, tearing pain was exhilarating" (p. 189).

terminology, a fixed symbol, which conveniently attaches itself to the escape and birth to freedom metaphors. The expanding symbol remains the rainbow or clipped arch symbol, those vague signs of the complete birth that Ursula strives for. Brown states that "the expanding symbol is a device far more appropriate for rendering an emotion, an idea, that by its largeness or its subtlety cannot become wholly explicit. The fixed symbol is almost entirely repetition" (p. 57). And Lawrence now begins to pound home the fixed symbol of separation with dogmatic insistence.

From the moment Ursula is (literally) born, both her helpless dependency and that significant "separateness" are emphasized. As a baby Ursula "had a separate being" (p. 209), yet she lived only for the return of her father at night. Naturally unaware of the dangerous psychological pitfall she skirts, she enjoys these early years with Will in ignorant bliss. However, their warm relationship occasionally is interrupted by alienating incidents, exemplified when he yells at her for trampling on the potatoes. The description of her helping him with the potato planting involves the same rhythmic use of "near, nearer" that has been evident in two crucial scenes with Will: his erotic sheaves scene with Anna and his attempted seduction of the girl from the Nottingham theater. Thus this scene with his young daughter both emphasizes that "rhythmic working up to culmination" of any emotional crisis, and also purposefully sounds like the two explicitly sexual scenes that involve his wife and the pick-up. Indeed, the description of the rhythmic action on the potato patch is more meaningful than the limited consciousness of either participant. It is the familiar language of sexual innuendo that rhythmically builds to its own climax as it highlights a relationship between two people in the great "creative flux":

She was excited and unused. She put in one potato, then rearranged it, to make it sit nicely. Some of the sprits were broken, and she was afraid. The responsibility excited her like a string tying her up. She could not help looking with dread at the string buried under the heaped-back soil. Her father was working nearer, stooping, working nearer. She was overcome by her responsibility. She put potatoes quickly into the cold earth. He came near. (p. 219)

After he yells at her, "the child was infinitely more shocked" (p. 220). Lawrence explains in *Psychoanalysis and the Unconscious,* as the metaphor of ontogeny continues: "There is as well the continually widening gap. A wonderful rich commun- ion, and at the same time a continually increasing cleavage" (p. 22). And the cleavage broadens with a statement that in retrospect becomes the single most repeated lesson that she learns as "an organic existentialist heroine" until she is born: "So very soon she came to believe in the outward malevolence that was against her" (p. 221). Gradually Ursula comes to re- sent her father, and she lapses "into the separate world of her- self" (p. 222). Thus just as Ursula communes with her father she is "at the same time extricating it (her) self into single, *sepa- rate,* independent existence. The one process of unison cannot go on without the other process of purified severance" *(Psycho- analysis and the Unconscious,* p. 22, my italics). One process cannot go on without the other – here is a concise explana- tion of the psychology of the rhythm in the second half of the novel. It is a rewording of the "vitalistic pull and flow" that I discussed earlier, and it explains why Ursula at various times goes *back* to her father, Skrebensky, Winifred, and idealized re- ligion after she apparently is free of their influence. This move- ment and counter-movement are a reflection of Lawrence's in- telligent awareness that organic sunderings are not made per- manent in the flash of some epiphany, but from the gradual pulsing to-and-fro of unconscious desire that ultimately purges a person of his devitalizing urge.

In *Psychoanalysis and the Unconscious* Lawrence further ex- plains that in the child exists the necessity to cleave back to the parent. In the novel, as in life, there is even more justification for the psychology of this rhythmic pattern. Ursula becomes entranced by the purposeful activity of her father, as a newly- resolved Will temporarily establishes an equilibrium within him- self and is able to work efficiently. In *Psychoanalysis and the Unconscious* Lawrence states that "at first the child cleaves back to the old source. It *clings and adheres*" (p. 22). I italicize that phrase because it conveniently relates to Ursula's daredevil,

symbolic jump in the water on her naked father's back. She barely manages to hang on, she almost kills him in the clinging attempt to live; but when they emerge after their glimpse of
death "still they were not separate" (p. 223). Ursula had almost
separated from her father, and only youthful tenacity and fear
holds her to Will. Yet that literal and metaphorical rift between
them continues to widen when he dangerously plays with her at
an amusement park. Unlike Miriam Leivers of *Sons and Lovers,*
the swinging scene enflames Ursula's senses; but her father's com-
pulsive acts are recognized as the sad self-tortures of a drowning man: "Her soul was dead towards him ... though still she
fought and continued to love him, but ever more coldly" (p.
223). Her "soul" here is not her "spirit", but the more encom-
passing essential self – that is, she now only goes through the
motions of a deep affection for her father. Finally, Will hits her
for a minor offense, and with echoes of the electricity imagery,
there is a short-circuit between them, as she "burned away her
connection with him" (p. 265). Ursula is free of her father; she
has completed her first sundering, for "her blazing heart was
fierce and unyielding .... She no longer belonged to him un-
questioned" (p. 265). Ursula, therefore, who slowly is undergoing her own birth, resembles the metaphorical embryo in
Psychoanalysis and the Unconscious, who "kicks away into independence. It stiffens its spine in the strength of its own private
and separate, inviolable existence. It will admit now of no tres-
pass. It is awake now in a new pride, a new self-assertion" (p.
24). And as Ursula rhythmically asserts herself forward, she
begins to emerge as embryo and woman.

Even before her final rupture with her father, the very process of leaving Cossethay is described as a bursting out of a narrow womb: "She found that the way to escape was easy. One
departed from the whole circumstance. ... So even as a girl of
twelve she was glad to burst the narrow boundary of Cossethay"
(p. 262). And Will's burnt-out connection with his daughter
recalls the vividly analogous incident of Will's uncle, Tom,
tearing the clothes off his daughter in the heat of anger. The
grandfather thus destroyed the conflicting relationship of abra-

sive opposition that he had attained with Anna, and substituted for it the temporarily cohesive electric contact made possible by Anna's and his own mutual awareness of the communion value of the seductive world of the barn. Yet Ursula dares not wait for reconciliation with her father through exposure to some new and beguiling environment. She has not stayed to have her clothes torn off, and instead she has torn the womb. Since she will be born from herself – it is *her own* womb she tears – the birth is slow and very painful.

Ursula has achieved a degree of "separateness" through the break with her father, and she has established the basic rhythm of sundering. However, she is not nearly the self-sufficient precursor of the creative unconscious birth that Lawrence will evolve. Her cutting of the parental umbilical cord precipitates a typical period of aimless, adolescent drifting and escapist dreams. She has romantic hallucinations and grandiose visions of her father, grandmother, the seasons, school, and herself. Soon Ursula seems to hear the Lawrence command – phrased in that metaphor of womb exit – to "move out of the intricately woven illusion of her life" (p. 266), for motivated by a stimulating period at high school, she ceases her daytime dreams. But as I indicated earlier, the rhythm of Ursula's consecutive sundering does not create any consistent momentum toward her birth. She is subject to extended slumps, and unfortunately she substitutes for the entire fabric of pubescent illusion the anti-Lawrentian image of a super-idealized, snobbish Christ. On only one day of the week, Ursula feels, is she able to sense the central direction towards her organic birth. The criticism that Lawrence has for this approach concerns the exclusive, idealistic nature of the idolatry: "But as yet, on Sunday, she was free, really free, free to be herself, without fear or misgiving. . . . Only the Sunday world existed" (p. 269). Ursula will learn that such freedom need not be restricted to Sunday.

Her belief in the mystical value of Christ and in the nonliteral application of the scriptures has Lawrence's blessing – as does her implicit criticism of the habituated emphasis on a history of Christ that stressed death rather than resurrection, that made "this rhythm of eternity in a ragged, inconsequential life" (p. 279). Lawrence believes in a "rhythm of eternity," an eternal rhythm of birth and death, and trial and error, but he bemoans (with Ursula) the fact that "it was becoming a mechanical action now, this drama: birth at Christmas for death at Good Friday" (p. 270). Ursula vacillates between extremes, between a belief only in the "Sunday world" (i.e., religion, visions), and a belief in the cold, visionless reality of the weekday world. She is unable to combine the two, and when she does, "she was ashamed of her religious ecstasy, and dreaded lest anyone should see it" (p. 284). She is most comfortable when she constructs and cherishes an enormously idealized image of Christ in her mind to substitute for the loss of her paternal attachment. We recall Lawrence's apt admonition: "What we are suffering from now is the restriction of the unconscious within certain ideal limits. The more we force the ideal the more we rupture the true movement" (*Psychoanalysis and the Unconscious*, p. 16). Ursula does not suffer this rupture for long, as she sunders herself alternately from the over-idealized Christ, from the non-mystical one, and then from all Christs altogether. She cannot combine the vision world and the weekday world, she is frustrated, and is "blowing about like the winds of heaven, undefined, unstated" (p. 282). But the timing of this imagery can be deceiving. In later sections of *The Rainbow,* Ursula really will be as "separate", as free as the wind is. Yet after her sunderings from an over-dependent father and various Christ images, she is separate only through default. That is, she has no idea about the responsibilities of her incipient freedom, and her liberty from attachments has barely more than a passing circumstantial relevance to her:

She became aware of herself, that she was a separate entity in the midst of an unseparated obscurity, that she must go somewhere, she must become something. And she was afraid, troubled. Why, oh why must one grow up, why must one inherit this heavy, numbing responsibility of living an undiscovered life? Out of the nothingness and the undifferentiated mass, to make something of herself! But what?   (p. 281)

The embryonic metaphor is all there: "separate", "she must become something", "must one grow up", "inherit", "undiscovered life". Ursula's fears here reflect her own unconscious realization that she is headed for the necessary trauma of rebirth. As though to answer Ursula's question in doctrinaire terms, Lawrence had asked in *Psychoanalysis and the Unconscious:* "... pain is a living reality, not merely a deathly. Why haven't we the courage for life pains?" (p. 21). And in a later essay he succinctly explains why these life pains of growth are necessary: "The living self has one purpose only: to come into its own fullness of being, as a tree comes into full blossom or a tiger into lustre."[2] That purpose must defy the pain – in fact, it must welcome it as the unmistakable sign of developing organic maturity.

Within this "unseparated obscurity" mentioned above, Ursula is forced to take a direction, and the author poses the question to her: "But whither?" (p. 281). It is towards a repetition of the psychology of family history, as Ursula takes a compromised solace in the physicality of a fleshly Christ that is the harbinger of Skrebensky's body. Lawrence's psychological analysis in *Psychoanalysis and the Unconscious* holds true for the rhythm of his fiction, as Lawrence talks of the need to "work out" your new self:

For though the unconscious is the creative element, and though, like the soul, it is beyond all law of cause and effect in its totality, yet in its processes of self-realization it follows the laws of cause and effect. The processes of cause and effect are indeed part of the working out of this incomprehensible self-realization of the individual unconscious.   (p. 16)

Here Lawrence recognizes the contributing function of heredity as a causative element in a person's realization of his creative unconscious, of his undiscovered birth potential. And the recognition explains not only the broad pattern of syntactical and situational similarities that the rhythm of the generations reveals, but also the nearly identical psychological problems that are

[2]   "Democracy", in *Phoenix*, p. 714.

dramatized. Obviously, Lawrence places the burden of his psychology on heredity rather than environment because he always emphasizes the healthy power of any instinctive response against the conditioned one. Thus the choice of a physical Jesus leading to a sensuous Skrebensky parallel those irrevocable decisions made by Ursula's mother, and grandmother before her. Both Lydia and Anna are more versatile and realistically perceptive than their more limited, semi-castrated husbands. But each woman was seduced primarily by the lure of the genuine animal quickness of her suitor, by the charismatic sensuous appeal reflected *either* in a fine body or the beguiling story of a mystical church. Lawrence does not need to be taught that the spirit can be as erotic as the flesh.

Thus the older Brangwen women were captivated by (and remain captive to) the blood intimacy offered by Tom and Will. It is certainly not surprising, if precedent or the point about heredity in Lawrence's essay have any value, that Ursula should fall before a similar enticement. This is not merely to say that Ursula is likely to be physically attracted by a virile male: it indicates her possible tendency to become seriously involved "on the physical level" with an individual far below her on Lawrence's abstract scale of "the creative unconscious". Yet while Lydia and Anna shut off their birth by marrying the blood-intimacy, Ursula only encounters it, first through her fleshly Jesus, and more extensively through her lover, Anton Skrebensky. The escape from this kind of delimiting marriage is part of the measure of her increased strength; that she is more powerful than mother and grandmother is eminently understandable in Lawrence's psychology of the embryo: "The intrinsic truth of every individual is the new unit of unique individuality which emanates from the fusion of the parent nuclei: This is the incalculable and intangible Holy Ghost each time – each individual his own Holy Ghost" *(Fantasia of the Unconscious,* p. 71). The Holy Ghost, quite simply, is that potent and invisible "otherness", that germ of unknown newness which makes Ursula able to resist the temptations to which her forebears succumb.

That sex does entrap, tease, and even falsify, that its uses are varied as its consequences are diverse is, indeed, a broad thematic strain in *The Rainbow*. Marvin Mudrick concisely sums up this theme when he calls *The Rainbow* "the first English novel to record the normality and significance of physical passion."[3] His choice of terms conveniently encompasses the realizations that Ursula gradually attains during the rhythm of her birth pains. His term "normality" I consider as the indication of the blanket awareness of the greatly motivating physical inclination in man; "blanket" because it covers every aspect of a person's life, from the apparently disparate experiences of a trip to the barn with a father, the picking of sheaves with a lover, to the rhapsodizing over a church. "Significance" refers to the recognition – and Ursula is expectedly slow to "recognize" – of the function such inclination has in a specific relationship. At different stages in her life she cannot recognize the dangerous role it plays in her relationship with her father, Winifred, and Skrebensky. But each time, as the rhythm always asserts itself behind the same psychology, she is strong enough to weather her confusion, survive the battle, and sunder herself ultimately from the force or object that attracts her. The psychology of the last half of the novel is a kind of "experiential brinksmanship", and the rhythm of the birth drive always threatens to halt with Ursula's capitulation to one force or the other.

Thus Ursula refines her ideal Jesus to a majestic sensuous deity that prepares for the fleshly coming of an even less spiritualized Skrebensky. Pursuing the cause and effect doctrine of the hereditary rhythm of the generations mentioned in *Psychoanalysis and the Unconscious* evidences further grounds for Ursula's abandonment of an over-idealized Christ. Her grandmother, Lydia, had briefly and desperately embraced a similar dream world, only to eventually abandon it forever. More graphically, Ursula's mother understandably has been discontent all along with

---

[3] "The Originality of *The Rainbow*", by Marvin Mudrick. Appeared in *D. H. Lawrence: A Collection of Critical Essays*, edited by Mark Spilka (Englewood Cliffs, N. J., 1963), p. 34. (From *Spectrum*, II, Winter 1959, pp. 3-28.)

Will's etherialized religion. Ursula picks up the outlines of this rhythm as she drops her masturbatory Gods, and she takes that crucial step toward the conventional, shallow, yet tangible replacement – Skrebensky. He opportunely arrives right after Lawrence's explicit reference to Ursula as not only physically frustrated, but also very much the young embryo: "So she wrestled through her dark days of confusion, soul-less, uncreated, unformed" (p. 286). Though she is taken in, as Lawrence phrases it, by the very directness of his physical presence (cf. Will), Lawrence dramatizes his meaning in *Psychoanalysis and the Unconscious* when he elaborates the metaphor of the child in the womb: "It must recoil clean upon itself, break loose from any attachment whatsoever. And then it must try its *power . . .*" (p. 27). When Ursula barely knows Skrebensky she decides that "she must ever prove her power" (p. 300). Skrebensky gives her ample opportunity.

From the start of their relationship, Ursula's developing creative unconscious urges her to triumph over Skrebensky, to attain complete mastery over his significantly poor powers of defense. What was merely a pattern of female initiative in the earlier generation now has accelerated into the crushing rhythm of complete female domination. The first episode of their love-making exhibits Ursula very much in charge, almost pitying in her treatment of him: "A hot drenching surge rose within her, she opened her lips to him, in pained, poignant eddies she drew him nearer, she let him come farther. . . . She heard him breathing heavily, strangely, beside her. A terrible and magnificent sense of his strangeness possessed her" (pp. 297–298). Thus we not only see Ursula's mastery here, but also her absolute naiveté, an unsophistication that still unequivocally feeds upon Skrebensky. That is, his heavy breathing is a reflection, naturally enough, of his sexual excitement, and he is strange to *Ursula* only because she has never seen a sexually aroused male before. Ursula masters him despite her inexperience because he is so obviously an inherently inadequate person. Witness the following conversation, which catches them in a characteristic moment. It might be charming, but it is not:

"Does he love her?"
"It's a year and a half he's been with her now."
"What was she like?"
"Emily? Little, shy-violent sort of girl with nice eyebrows."
Ursula meditated this. It seemed like real romance of the outer world.
"Do all men have lovers?" she asked, amazed at her own temerity. But her hand was still fastened with his, and his face still had the same *unchanging fixity of outward calm.*
"They're always mentioning some amazing fine woman or other, and getting drunk to talk about her. Most of them dash up to London the moment they are free."
"What for?"
"To some amazing fine woman or other."
"What sort of woman?"
"Various. Her name changes pretty frequently as a rule. One of the fellows is a perfect maniac. He keeps a suit-case always ready, and the instant he is at liberty, he bolts with it to the station, and changes in the train. No matter who is in the carriage, off he whips his tunic, and performs at least the top half of his toilet."
Ursula quivered and wondered.   (p. 296, my italics)

What is interesting here is not the delineation of Ursula's ingenuousness played off against Skrebensky's relative experience; novels are replete with those scenes from *Clarissa* to the publishing of *Sister Carrie* fifteen years before *The Rainbow.* The power of the scene comes from the evocation of Skrebensky's superficial egotism complementing, stimulating, and making erotic contact with Ursula's tempting innocence. They are both blissfully unaware of the processes that are working inside of them, and Skrebensky has even managed to fool himself. The repetition of the "amazing fine woman" indicates an excitement of his own that he is unwilling to admit explicitly to himself or to Ursula. This is the only conversation with Ursula in which Skrebensky will appear as more knowledgeable than Ursula, and even here he is one big self-deluding facade hiding his insecurity. "The unchanging fixity of outward calm" – Lawrence dislikes Skrebensky enough to give him away with incisive narrative intrusion.

It is of great importance to not only catch Lawrence's repeated criticism of Skrebensky in the novel, but also to realize that Ursula does not act out of egotistical impulses during her pro-

tracted destruction of him. Her frequent triumphs over Skrebensky, of which the first kissing scene is a mild example, are
merely the rhythmic "limbering up" of her creative unconscious,
the working out of its desires for the unfettered freedom of birth
on its most rudimentary level. Unless this fact is understood,
Ursula's treatment of Skrebensky would be considered manipu-
lative rather than instinctive, and selfish rather than necessary
for survival. In *Psychoanalysis and the Unconscious* Lawrence
adamantly argues:

> It is perhaps difficult for us to realize the strong, blind power of the
> unconscious on its first plane of activity. It is something quite dif-
> ferent from what we call *egoism* – which is really mentally derived
> – for the ego is merely the sum total of what we conceive ourselves
> to be. The powerful pristine subjectivity of the unconscious on its
> first plane is, on the other hand, the root of all our consciousness
> and being, darkly tenacious.   (p. 28)

It is the "root of our being"; to deny it would be to deny growth.
In a letter to his friend Edward Garnett, Lawrence emphasizes the
psychology of the rhythmic struggle, and, in effect, warns us
against castigating Ursula for an impulse which must be mani-
fested in order for her to reach the desired end of conscious
being: "You mustn't look for the old stable *ego* of the character.
There is another ego, according to whose action the individual is
unrecognizable, and passes through, as it were, allotropic states
which it needs a deeper sense than any other we've been used
to exercise to discover."[4] Ursula, therefore, throughout her killing of Skrebensky, both is submitting to her intense physical
desires and simultaneously crushing him to death through the
expression of the creative unconscious drive for birth. The passage through allotropic states mentioned to Garnett represents
the outline of Ursula's sundering transitional experiences to the
fulfilling birth at the end of the novel. The passage – ultimately
sort of "rites of passage" – creates the psychology of the
rhythm of sundering which progessively "separates" Ursula until she becomes "recognizable" in the terms of the above letter. Ursula meets her match in Rupert Birkin in *Women In Love*,

---

[4] *Letters,* p. 282.

and there the sense of one-sided battle that characterizes her relationship with Skrebensky will be replaced by a creative atmosphere of commingling, connection, fruitful tension, and necessary conflict.[5] But as for Skrebensky in *The Rainbow,* Ursula continues to break him as Lawrence's essay implied she would. The third woman in the novel to be described as an open-flower, she is a venus fly-trap to her lover:

> Like a flower shaking and wide-opened in the sun, she tempted him and challenged him . . . it was begun now, this passion, and must go on, the passion of Ursula to know her own maximum self, limited and so defined against him. She could limit and define herself against him, the male, she could be her maximum self, female, oh female, triumphant for one moment in exquisite assertion against the male, in supreme contradistinction to the male.   (pp. 300–301)

Note the forward rhythm of the language: "must go on. . . . to know her own maximum self. . . . she could be her maximum self." Once the rhythmic progress starts for a person to know his "maximum self" – that is, his full self, any challenge in the way of that organic process must be met with all the power at one's disposal. Why know one's own "maximum self" (which is certainly an excellent phrase for a metaphorically complete embryo)? Lawrence responds in *Fantasia of the Unconscious:* "And only at his maximum does an individual surpass all his derivative elements and become purely himself" (p. 71). Thus only at her maximum can Ursula get beyond her inherited qualities ("derivative elements") and refuse to capitulate to the erotic onslaught of Skrebensky. The whole of *The Rainbow* is the outline of the effort to have at least one Brangwen become "purely himself".

Skrebensky's delimiting military oocupation forces him to briefly leave Ursula, and when he returns he explicitly reveals himself to her as a conventional fool with a neo-Benthamite

---

[5]   The pattern of "rhythmic progress" in *Women In Love* does not resemble the pattern in *The Rainbow.* In *Women In Love* an already "born" Ursula essentially must learn two things: to allow the complete separatist self-assertion of Birkin, and to permit Birkin to express his unconventional need for Gerald Crich. She learns the first lesson after much conflict by the "Ex-

conversation about war and national service. But a maturing Ursula is no longer blindly attracted by Skrebensky's military background. Skrebensky believes in his romantic, *noblesse-oblige* image of himself as patriotic servant, and he sadly resembles the man in *Psychoanalysis and the Unconscious* who, "once he has built himself in the shape of any ideal. . . . will go to any logical length rather than abandon his ideal corpus" (p. 12). Skrebensky firmly states his ideal: "I belong to the nation and must do my duty by the nation" (p. 309). Lawrence's destructive characterization of him and his ideal is the author's way of paying back the "nation" for its vicious holding of him for conscriptive purposes at the time this novel was written. Conversations like the following with an incredibly *childish* Skrebensky force Ursula toward further sundering movement; they bring back that sense of "separateness" we previously watched her dissipate twice – once after her break with Will, and again after her flirtation with the idealized Jesus. Ursula starts the questioning, and the sundering movement begins once more:

"Would you like to go to war?"
"I? Well it would be exciting. If there were a war I would want to go." A strange distracted feeling came over her, a sense of potent unrealities.
"Why would you want to go?"
"I should be doing something, it would be genuine. It's a sort of toy-life as it is."
"But what would you be doing if you went to war?"
"I would be making railways or bridges, working like a nigger."
"But you'd only make them to be pulled down again when the armies had done with them. It seems just as much a game."
"If you call war a game."
"What is it?"
"It's about the most serious business there is, fighting."
A hard sense of separateness came over her.
(p. 308, my italics)

---

curse" chapter, and she never learns the second. This relatively simple scheme is a testament to the less exhaustive nature of the rhythmic struggles that Ursula undergoes in *Women In Love*. That is, the crises of Ursula's post-natal development in the later novel center around two distinct places, while the whole history of Ursula in *The Rainbow* is the continuous rhythm of crisis.

Not only the thrust of his remarks, but the rhythm of his syntax (i.e., "I would be making railways or bridges.") indicates that after Tom and Will Brangwen, we now have the most extreme version of the boy-man in Lawrence's novel. Skrebensky obviously ignores the exhortation which Lawrence makes in *Fantasia of the Unconscious:* "Let them be soldiers, but as individuals, not machine units" (p. 123). This conversation, incidentally, comes after Lawrence stresses Skrebensky's juvenile, over-sympathetic stance with these lines: "To him this was bitter, that she was so radiant and satisfied (p. 302). . . . Was she going to make this easy triumph over him. . . . It was agony to him, seeing her swift and cleancut and virgin" (pp. 302-303). Thus the act of courtship to him, like war, is a game in which he must have petty triumphs over the girl, despise her victory, and feel unnecessary jealousy over her own power. The ego that he cannot satisfy with Ursula he will try to nourish in the military tradition that takes him to India.

Ursula never completely loses this sense of separateness from Skrebensky throughout the remainder of their destructive affair. Immediately after her conversation above with Skrebensky, Lawrence symbolically accentuates Ursula's newly developed feeling of alienation from him, as a developing Ursula meets a newborn "Ursula". She descends alone into the cabin of a barge; as Skrebensky waits with characteristic jealous impatience for her return, she warmly engages an older couple in conversation and plays with their still unnamed baby girl. The parents decide to call the baby "Ursula" – Lawrence's pointed comment right after Ursula's "sense of separateness" from Skrebensky that Ursula herself is undergoing a baptismal awakening into the realms of organic being. Ursula also gives away the necklace that her *father* (from whom she has sundered herself) gave her. It is also significant that her communication with these people, her spontaneous exchanges of affection, contain more genuine, good-natured warmth than we have seen her experience with Skrebensky. This incident of Ursula's positive inter-action with the family is Lawrence's means of illustrating the sensitivity that Ursula is capable of when the right opportunity presents itself.

In short, because she is being born, and therefore since she frequently must wrench herself rudely from devitalizing attachments, she has been shown for most of the novel as involved in the headstrong rhythm of progressive sundering. The Ursula that emerges from the cabin is glowing, self-sufficient, and geared for the long struggle ahead. On deck all the self-protectively pompous Skrebensky can manage is, "The woman had been a servant, I'm sure of that" (p. 314) – an ironic comment by Lawrence after Skrebensky's own ardent expressions of chauvinistic service. "Ursula winced" to Skrebensky's remark, and as they hurry home Skrebensky wonders why he cannot love the body *and* soul of Ursula: "Why could not he himself desire a woman so? Why did he never really want a woman, not with the whole of him: never loved, never worshipped, only just physically wanted her" (p. 315). Lawrence writes in *Fantasia of the Unconscious* that "sex as an end in itself is a disaster, a vice" (p. 214), and Skrebensky is about to pay the disastrous price.

The price will be paid on the passionate battlefield of a sexual war, where the issues can be presented clearly and resolved most emphatically. As the physical desires of Skrebensky and Ursula understandably mount, and as Ursula's awareness of Skrebensky's limitations increases, they prepare themselves for the first of three devastating encounters under the moon – again, that symbol of separatist self-assertion: "The moon is, as it were, the pole of our particular terrestial *volition* in the universe" *(Fantasia of the Unconscious, p. 184)*. They dance together in a suggestive setting, passions ignite, Skrebensky wants her body while Ursula begs for the moon. The dance is Ursula's more potent version of her mother's dance of annihilation; the following references in the description to "flux" and "trance of motion" are versions of the "polarized flux", "pulsing to-and-fro", and "movement and steadying movement" to which Lawrence has referred previously:

At the touch of her hand on his arm, his consciousness melted away from him. He took her into his arms, as if into the sure, subtle power of his will, and they became one movement, one dual movement, dancing on the slippery grass. It would be endless, this movement, it would continue for ever. It was his will and her will locked in a trance of motion, two wills locked in one motion, yet never fusing, never yielding one to the other. It was a glaucous, intertwining, delicious flux and contest in flux. (p. 316)

But it will end, for there is really no contest here – the flux of movement will give way to stasis. Lawrence writes "and still he had not got her" (p. 318), which is the same language used in the pulsing rhythm of chase during the sheaves scene: "Were they never to meet ... why was he held away from her" (pp. 118-119). Unlike Will, however, Anton never overtakes his girl. Mark Spilka stresses the significance of these moon scenes in a very provocative way. He explains that Ursula resembles both Diana, the Moon goddess who protects woman, and the daughter of Aphrodite, whom "Lawrence calls the goddess of dissolution and death".[6] Thus as Ursula seeks rhythmic communion with the moon, she asserts her triumphant femininity as a woman whose psychology calls upon her to destroy the oppressive weight on her (cf. "Skrebensky like a load-stone weighed on her", p. 317) and as a mythical goddess (beyond psychology, as it were) whose very triumph is insured by her name and the moon environment. Spilka remarks that "in each of these scenes, she taunts Skrebensky to take her under the moonlight and though he complies, he feels each time some sort of proof is being put upon him and that death is the penalty for failure."[7] And it is nearly death ("He knew he would die" p. 319), for one cannot love a goddess and then lure her to India, and a spiritually emasculated man cannot have real intercourse with a woman as powerful as Ursula. Ultimately he is allowed to live only because he learns to live without her.

Psychoanalysis and the Unconscious provides an additional meaning for the psychology of the rhythm of the moon scenes. I have noted previously that the moon is for Lawrence the symbol of individuality, of inviolable separateness. Also, Ursula's de-

---

[6]   Spilka, p. 112.
[7]   Lawrence proves in Fantasia how literally right Spilka is: "To the individual the act of coition is a great psychic experience of tremendous importance. On this vital individual experience the life and very being of the individual largely depends." (p. 141)

struction of Skrebensky occurs under a symbolic moon which reflects an additional psychological source of Ursula's rhythmic annihilation of him. Ursula never really "loves" Skrebensky because she is always able to "know" him – she pins down his core from all sides. Later she states that "not in any side did he lead into the unknown" (p. 473).[8] Ursula's intercourse with Skrebensky is always deadly because is probes his eminently knowable self. In his famous Poe essay, Lawrence asserts that "to *know* a living thing is to kill it",[9] and in *Psychoanalysis and the Unconscious* he significantly states: "Of that reflected or moonlove derived from the head, that spurious form of love which predominates today, we do not speak here. It has its root in the *idea*, the beloved is a mental objective, endlessly appreciated, criticized, scrutinized, exhausted. This has nothing to do with the active unconscious" (p. 30). That is, Ursula's sexual meetings with Skrebensky are created in his terms; their sex cannot get beyond that "spurious form of love" because he has no beyond to offer her: "She stood for some moments in the overwhelming luminosity of the moon. . . . Looking at him, at his shadowy, unreal, wavering presence a sudden lust seized her, to lay hold of him and tear him and make him into nothing. . . . He waited there beside her like a shadow" (p. 319). "His shadowy, unreal, wavering presence" – the same unsubstantial way Will looked to a pregnant Anna and Tom to a pregnant Lydia in two earlier scenes. Ursula is now pregnant with herself. Skrebensky's presence here is both an insult to her creative unconscious powers – mythic and otherwise – and a temptation for her to use them. The penetrating force of Ursula's struggle for consummation asserts itself under the influence of Skrebensky and the goddess moon, and the porous Skrebensky has no force to return.

In *Psychoanalysis and the Unconscious*, Lawrence expands his metaphor of the growing embryo making contact with the out-

---

[8] "But the love will be a nest of scorpions unless it is overshadowed by a little fear of your further purpose, a living *belief* in your going beyond her, into futurity." *Fantasia*, p. 219.

[9] "Edgar Allan Poe", in *Studies In Classic American Literature*, p. 70.

side world: "So long as the force meets its polarized response all is well. When a force flashes and has no response, there is devastation" (p. 24). And he is more explicit in *Fantasia of the Unconscious* about the rhythms of this exchange: "So it is in sex relation. There is a threefold result. First the flash of pure sensation and of real electricity. Then there is the *birth* of an entirely new state of blood in each partner. And then there is the liberation" (p. 214). But note the sexual relation between Skrebensky and Ursula: no electricity, no freedom, and no liberation beyond her one-sided victory over him. Not the flash of electricity, but only the crush of iron and the dissolution of salt:

But hard and fierce she had fastened upon him, cold as the moon and burning as a fierce salt. Till gradually his warm, soft iron yielded, and she was there fierce, corrosive, seething with his destruction, seething like some cruel, corrosive salt around the last substance of his being, destroying him, destroying him in the kiss. And her soul crystallized with triumph, and his soul was dissolved with agony and annihilation. So she held him there, the victim, consumed, annihilated. She had triumphed: he was not any more. (p. 320)

"Destruction", "dissolved", "consumed", "annihilation" – for Ursula goes right through *him*, and the reversal of sexual roles implied by that metaphor is justified by a language that describes the rape of a male: "she had fastened upon him. . . . his warm soft iron yielded. . . . so she held him there". There is certainly not the "liberation" Lawrence talked about in *Fantasia of the Unconscious*. There is pure slavery: "As a distinct male he had no core. . . . He would be subject now" (p. 321). Eugene Goodheart surprisingly sees little danger to the bodily self from the presence of the stronger sexual "other" in *The Rainbow*, from the presence of a well-defined and mastering male or female counter-force.[10] Yet this is not right, for the failures of the dramatically weaker force in Lawrence's fiction lead to this less vitalized person's collapse on all levels of existence. Which is in Lawrence's psychology as it should be: Lawrence claims that those repeated rhythms of life do not merely create occasional depres-

[10]   Eugene Goodheart, *The Utopian Vision of D. H. Lawrence* (Chicago, 1963), p. 128.

sion or anxiety, but also chart the progress to nothing less than
either a life leading to organic compromise or meaningful rebirth. Every moon scene tears a little more at Skrebensky's body,
and his utter physical weakness on the day of his final departure from Ursula, or his sobbing, and lastly his "burned-out"
eyes all indicate that for Ursula to have continued "annihilating
him" would mean more than simply the destruction of his confidence with women. Skrebensky's decline may be considered
on a naturalistic level as expectedly psychosomatic, and on a
symbolic level as a result of the mythic aggressions of Ursula.
He has intercourse with a goddess and a woman, and he is not the
man for either job.

Thus again Ursula breaks a bond ("she knew she broke him")
and surmounts one of the birth barriers that necessitate the
rhythms of her passionate struggle into conscious being. Yet she
is also adrift for a third time, and though she moves forward in
her understanding and mastery of Skrebensky's weakness, and
in the realization of her unconscious self, the movement is not
completed though the tempo increases: "For the whole point
about the true unconscious is that it is all the time moving forward, beyond the range of its own fixed laws and habits"
(Psychoanalysis and the Unconscious, p. 16). It is precisely the
inability of earlier generations of Brangwens to move beyond
that fixed horizon of blood-intimacy and domesticity that hin-
ders their own process of self-realization. And at this stage in
their relationship that fixed metaphor of "birth from oneself"
describes the situation of Ursula and Skrebensky very accurately.
Skrebensky has given up: "At the bottom of his heart his self,
the soul that aspired and had true hope of self-effectuation, lay
as dead, stillborn, a dead weight in his womb" (p. 326). Ursula
still is *unborn* – not stillborn – and the phrasing of her birth
condition purposely sounds a rhetoric of potentiality, of things
to come, of lives to be: "Her life was only partial at this time,
never did she live completely (p. 331) .... Her life at this time
was unformed" (p. 334). When Skrebensky goes overseas for
the first time, Ursula senses both her uncomfortable "separation" from his body, and her own developing "separateness". But

she also engages in a series of "growth" interludes that indicate she is fighting a losing battle with her physical dependency on him. The next section of the novel traces the psychology of the rhythm of Ursula's experience with four distinct sunderings, as she rejects first a perverted sexual relationship, second, a commitment to a machine civilization, third, the confining atmosphere of her family, and finally, the destructive use of her own human will.

After the first of her frustrating episodes with Skrebensky under the moon, Ursula is ripe for her affair with the lesbian, Winifred. Winifred unsubtly embodies an anti-religious, feminist intellectualism, which Lawrence adamantly associated with Bertrand Russell and the Cambridge group. Lawrence is as disturbed by "politicized" women of this sort as Yeats, and he is just as explicit in his denunciation of them. After her triumphant but unsatisfying clash with the meek Skrebensky, Ursula is attracted to Winifred's ideal, challenging conception of God as a lion, as powerful Moloch. In the essence of this ideal Ursula mistakenly identifies the organic manliness she found lacking in Skrebensky. Indeed, she is described very much like Skrebensky — the regimentation is terribly similar:

To Ursula she had always given pleasure, because of her clear, decided, yet graceful appearance. She carried her head high, a little thrown back, and Ursula thought there was a look of nobility in the way she twisted her smooth brown hair upon her head. She always wore clean, attractive, well-fitting blouses, and a well-made skirt. Everything about her was so well-ordered, betraying a fine, clear spirit, that it was a pleasure to sit in her class.   (p. 335)

But Lawrence warns us about Winifred in *Psychoanalysis and the Unconscious:*

This motivating of the passional sphere from the ideal is the final peril of human consciousness. It is the death of all spontaneous, creative life, and the substituting of the mechanical principle. It is obvious that the ideal becomes a mechanical principle, if it be applied to the affective soul as a fixed motive. An ideal established in control of the passional soul is no more and no less than a supreme machine principle.   (pp. 11–12)

Winifred is a perverted, mechanized form of masculine female; her deviate actions in the pool with Ursula, her indomitable support of women's rights, and her sinister attachment to Ursula's Uncle Tom all suggest a woman whose creative unconscious has been distorted by an automaton willingness to rule herself by quasi-ideal, yet rigidly defined motives. The psychology of her life is deathly and its rhythm is deadening. Besides the compensating reason for her attraction to Winifred, Ursula is further drawn to her because Winifred's articulate description of men ironically approximates the uncomfortable quality of Ursula's experience with Skrebensky: "They are all impotent, they can't take a woman. They come to their own idea every time, and take that" (p. 342). Winifred describes here the whole boy-man psychology that is reiterated through Tom, Will, and Skrebensky: they are all men who found that they could "not get free" even when they have intercourse with the woman they desire, for they base so much of their freedom on the ego-boosting value of the act itself. As Lawrence critically remarks in his *Letters:* "When a man takes a woman, he is *merely* repeating a known reaction upon himself, not seeking a new reaction, a discovery."[11] Thus Lawrence is one of the first novelists to describe the psychology of the rhythm of masturbatory intercourse, and Skrebensky is at the center of the description.

With Skrebensky abroad and Winifred away on a trip, a stasis settles over Ursula in which little substantial change takes place in her. She neither slides back into a more intense relationship with Winifred, nor moves forward in the consistent rhythm of her birth: "It was the terrible core of all her suffering, that she was always herself. Never could she escape that" (p. 342). It is the subtlety of this statement that precisely because Ursula is herself – rather, will *become herself* – that she does escape the suffering. But she can sunder herself from Winifred, and she does this by marrying her off to the supreme mechanist, her Uncle Tom. Lawrence's extended description of the colliery system over which Tom rules is important because it dramatizes the

11 *Letters,* p. 319.

kind of environment that the "hope" on the last page of the novel must eventually destroy. In addition, this process of mining is decribed as providing life and freedom for Tom and Winifred, and thus their mechanical birth is contrasted to the incipient organic birth of Ursula. Tom reigns over a cruelly modern equivalent of "Uncle Tom's Cabin", an environment in which colliers are dirt-infested coal slaves, unable to summon up the communal activity needed to improve their squalid conditions. As supervisor, Tom mechanizes their fate to extract the greatest material reward. Lawrence writes about Tom and Winifred:

His real mistress was the machine, and the real mistress of Winifred was the machine. She too, Winifred, worshipped the impure abstraction, the mechanisms of matter. There, there, in the machine, in service of the machine, was she free from the clog and degradation of human feeling. There, in the monstrous mechanism that held all matter, living or dead, in its service, did she achieve her consummation and her perfect unison, her immortality. (p. 349)

But really not "free from the clog and degradation of human feeling"; instead, free from all affirmational feeling, free from the pain and glory of the rhythms of life that Ursula experiences in a non-mechanical manner. Winifred's "unison" here is with the sterile, unfeeling ideas of impure abstractions and ruthless materialism; she is justly rewarded in marriage with a person who is the living embodiment of her own deranged devotions. She will be able to continue the rhythms of her life with him in machine comfort. Lawrence echoes this view of Winifred in *Psychoanalysis and the Unconscious:* "Man has invented his own automatic principles, and he works himself according to them, like any little mechanic inside the works" (p. 12). The essay also suggests Tom's brutal organization of his colliers, an organization predicated on Tom's belief that "one man or another–it does not matter very much" (p. 347).

The mind is the dead end of life. But it has all the mechanical force of the non-vital universe. It is a great dynamo of super-mechanical force. Given the will as accomplice, it can even arrogate its machine-motions and automizations over the whole of life, till every tree becomes a clipped teapot and every man a useful mechanism.

(Psychoanalysis and the Unconscious, p. 47)

Ursula learns from her experience with Winifred and Tom, and she appropriates that organic knowledge as sustenance for her impending birth. For when she visits Tom and Winifred at Wiggiston, she observes enough about the horrors of machine life so that "it was in these weeks that Ursula grew up. . . . She stayed to get rid of Winifred" (p. 350). The combination of "grew up" and "get rid of" is a summary of the psychology of rhythm in this section of the novel. "Get rid of" refers explicitly to one of the necessary sunderings Ursula must undergo. "Grew *up*" – I put the emphasis on the second term, for the growth is not completed. She grows up enough to now consider sundering herself from the original womb of her parents.

Ursula's departure from her family – as the rhythm comes home – is something more than the traditional voyage away of the ambitious young female. Her ambition is motivated by a proper sensitivity to the life process itself, and Lawrence makes this clear in *Psychoanalysis and the Unconscious*: "We have to try to recognize the true nature and then leave the unconscious itself to prompt new movement and new being – the creative progress" (p. 16). Lawrence dramatizes the permissive nature of this statement with the period of Ursula's mistakes about the church, Winifred, Skrebensky, etc. The "creative progress" could be the title of the Ursula section of the novel: it summarizes the developmental quality of the rhythm of Ursula's sundering, and the life-creating force that the sunderings represent. Ursula leaves home because she finally recognizes the "true nature" of the limiting family atmosphere, and her departure "prompts new movement" (i.e., birth movement) by thrusting her into the enlightening and uncomfortable position of school-teacher. Ursula's desire for a job, therefore, coincides with a shocked awareness of her unstimulating environment at home. She already has left her father, and now she acutely criticizes a mother who has cut off her own birth with the achievement of domesticity:

Mrs. Brangwen was so complacent, so utterly fulfilled in her breeding. She would not have the existence at all of anything but the immediate, physical, common things. Ursula, inflamed in soul, was

suffering all the anguish of youth's reaching for some unknown
ordeal, that it can't grasp, can't even distinguish or conceive.

(p. 352)

Thus Ursula's embryonic push for the unknown is played off
against her mother's compromised security. But there is no
foolishly sanguine de-emphasis on Ursula's depression and feelings of uncertainty about where she is going when she is without Skrebensky, Winifred, and her parents. There is the same metaphor, but used for a very unhappy girl: "The tiny, vivid germ
that contained the bud of her real self, her real love, was killed,
she would go on growing as a plant, she would do her best to
produce her minor flowers, but her leading flower was dead
before it was born, all her growth was the conveying of a corpse
of hope" (p. 356, my italics). Her letter of advice from her high
school mistress continues the novel's central metaphor in a
pompous tone of academic jargon: "I most strongly urge and
advise you to keep up your studies always with the intention of
taking a degree. That will give you a qualification and a position
in the world, and will give you *more scope to choose your own
way....* I shall be glad indeed to know that one more of my
girls has provided for herself the means of *freedom to choose
for herself*" (p. 357, my italics). Ursula is bored enough to leave
home, and the extended, bitter quarrel with her family over her
proposed teaching functions make this crucial break more
symbolic and substantial. And when Ursula mails the applica-
tions, the metaphors return: "She felt as if already she was out
of the reach of her father and mother (p. 363) .... she existed
now as a separate social individual (p. 363)... she knew she
was free – she had broken away from him" (p. 364). On her
way to the job for the first time, the birth pains get very explicit:
"She was being carried forward into her new existence. Her heart
burned with pain and suspense, as if something were cutting her
living tissue" (p. 368). It has been cutting that post-embryonic
embryo inside her since she was literally born. Now she carries the
pain to school.

Ursula's teaching job represents Ursula's necessary excursion
into the mechanical man's world of brutal will. The description

of her experience is filled with an admirable display of Lawrence's gift of stylized portraiture. For instance, Ursula's first meeting with a male teacher reads right out of *Alice in Wonderland,* as the flexible, sensitive rhythms of Ursula's life clash in a ludicrous way with the dogmatic, mechanical rhythm of the man:

"Am I early?" she asked.
The man looked first at a little clock, then at her. His eyes seemed to be sharpened to needlepoints of vision.
"Twenty-five past," he said. "You're the second to come. I'm first this morning."
Ursula sat down gingerly on the edge of a chair, and watched his thin red hands rubbing away on the white surface of the paper, then pausing, pulling up a corner of the sheet, peering, and rubbing away again. There was a great heap of curled white-and-scribbled sheets on the table.
"Must you do so many?" asked Ursula.
Again the man glanced up sharply. He was about thirty or thirty-three years old, thin, greenish, with a long nose and a sharp face. His eyes were blue, and sharp as points of steel, rather beautiful, the girl thought.
"Sixty-three," he answered.
"So many!" she said, gently. Then she remembered.
"But they're not all for your class are they?" she added.
"Why aren't they?" he replied, a fierceness in his voice.
Ursula was rather frightened by his mechanical ignoring of her, and his directness of statement. It was something new to her. She had never been treated like this before, as if she did not count, as if she were addressing a machine. (pp. 369–370)

Only when Ursula briefly compromises a life and also becomes a machine (cf. "something went click in her soul", p. 398) is she able to exist in school. At school, the teacher Ursula receives an extended lesson on the dangers and power of the human "will". The administrators of the school would have Ursula ignore the inclinations of her own soul struggling into consciousness, and rather achieve iron discipline in her classroom through the imposition of cruel, willful power. The "will", when it combines with the mind, is the "hateful instrument" that Lawrence emphasized in his description of Winifred and Tom. In *Psychoanalysis and the Unconscious,* Lawrence notes: "The will is indeed the faculty which every individual possesses from the very moment of conception, for exhorting a certain control over the vital and automatic processes of his own evolution" (p. 47). Ursula does prevent briefly the further "evolution" of herself; it is unnecessary to trace her painfully gradual recognition of the horrors of "will" as used in the class-room. Lawrence belabors this recognition, and it will suffice to quote a characteristically insistent paragraph. A disillusioned Ursula learns that:

The first great task was to reduce sixty children to one state of mind or being. This state must be produced automatically, through the *will* of the teacher, and the *will* of the whole school authority, imposed upon the *will* of the children. The point was that the headmaster and the teachers should have one *will* in authority, which should bring the *will* of the children into accord. But the headmaster was narrow and exclusive. The *will* of the teachers could not agree with his, their separate *wills* refused to be so subordinated.

(p. 382, my italics)

Learning processes like Ursula's in school are part of the necessary life pains that Lawrence insists we must all undergo, as the embryo continues to tear from within: "She had paid a great price out of her own soul, to do this. It seemed as if a great flame had gone through her and burnt her sensitive tissue" (p. 405). She makes friends with an appealing but conventionally predictable suffragette, Maggie Schofield. Lawrence distinguishes between the two by revealing Maggie as the liberal who believes in the vote, and Ursula as the radical who really wants to get at the root: "To Ursula the vote was never a reality. She had within her the strange, passionate knowledge of religion and living far transcending the limits of the automatic system that contained the vote. But her fundamental, organic knowledge had as yet to take form and rise to utterance" (p. 406). Yes, Lawrence's emphasis on rebirth and organic being is embarrassing here, unless one's faith in the Lawrentian system is incredibly naive: in the praise which is implicit in Ursula's lack of belief in the vote, one must project ahead and imagine the unfortunate situation of potential voters spurning the establishment not because they want to change it, but because they await their own mystical

awareness. It is this kind of unconcern about the political framework – that is, about whether to change *or* accept it, that combines with a sometimes hysterical emphasis on that "passionate
knowledge of religion" of the select which slides Lawrence into
periods of modified Fascism later in life. Ursula now enters the
second "Widening Circle", as "Ursula broke from that form of
life wherein Maggie must remain enclosed" (p. 412). For the
politically minded, however, the circle noticeably has constrict-
ed.

That Ursula has struggled forward towards her birth since her
literal birth is, indeed, an understatement about the force of the
novel's rhythm. She progressively has sundered herself from
father, idealistic church, family, perverted love, and mechanized
will. She rejects the temptation of Anthony Schofield – sort
of a young Tom Brangwen – realizing that "his animal presence is all he has to offer" (p. 416). She has fought very hard to
make whatever birth movement she can, and Lawrence pre-
dicts in *Fantasia of the Unconscious* that it frequently is difficult
to get out of the womb: "And the struggling youth or maid cannot emerge unless by the energy of all powers, he can never
emerge if the whole mass of the world and the tradition of love
hold him back" (p. 150). Only the persistent Skrebensky holds
her back, and because of some foreshadowing Lawrentian imagery, it is obvious that the break with her "knowable" lover
is not far away: "Ultimately and finally, she must go on and on
seeking the goal that she knew she did draw nearer to" (p. 417).
As she travels on and on, the appropriateness of Lawrence's two
chapter headings, "The Widening Circle", is more apparent, as
is the rainbow symbol for birth, when Lawrence writes in *Fantasia of the Unconscious*: "The inanimate universe rests absolutely
on the life circuit of living creatures, is built upon the *arch*
which spans the duality of living beings (i.e., 'duality' = sympathetic and separatist stance)" (p. 189). Thus Lawrence stresses
the circular nature of Ursula's travels: "She saw herself travel-
ling round a circle, only an *arc* of which remained to complete.
Then, she was in the open, like a bird tossed into mid-air, a bird

that has learned in some measure to fly.... Come college and she would have broken from the confines of all the life she had known" (p. 417). Here Lawrence describes Ursula as more than a voyaging female Ulysses out of Tennyson – she also partakes of the Dedalus myth; only Skrebensky keeps her rhythm on the ground. Again, the fact that *Ursula*, not Lydia or Anna, can be described in these hyperbolic metaphorical terms is, of course, a key to that significant individuality of Ursula. Neither her mother nor grandmother, for all their womanly shrewdness and shreds of Shavian life-force could break the constricting bonds of the blood-intimacy that they married. Though Ursula flirts with these dangers from her father, Skrebensky, and Schofield, she ultimately resists their threats. Lawrence's metaphor in *Psychoanalysis and the Unconscious* of the child has great relevance for the broad outline of Ursula's individualized rhythm:

The nature of the infant is not just a new permutation-and-combination of elements contained in the natures of the parents. There is in the nature of the infant that which is utterly unknown in the natures of the parents. And this something is the unanalyzable, undefinable, reality of individuality. (p. 14)

And this something is why Lawrence spends more time on Ursula than anyone else in the novel.

Yet emancipated woman, world traveller, what is the significance of Ursula's *own* realization that such imagery is appropriate to describe herself? It represents Ursula's recognition that a change has taken place in her, a crucial conscious awareness that her consecutive sunderings have nearly released her and produced a new individual: "What was true of her ten years ago was not true now" (p. 419). She senses for herself the responsibility of her imminent birth: "Out of the far, far space there drifted slowly in her a passionate unborn yearning... all her unborn soul was crying for the unrisen dawns.... That which she was, positively, was dark and unrevealed, it could not come forth" (p. 437). In short, the process of sundering, of negative reaction, is exhausting to Ursula; she yearns for the respite of birth, for now "she could only stiffen in rejection, in rejection" (p. 437). In *Psychoanalysis and the Unconscious* Lawrence writes accordingly about the embryo: "The little back has an amazing power once it stiffens itself. In the lumbar ganglion the unconscious now vibrates tremendously in the activity of sundering" (p. 23). Ursula immediately gets her desired feeling of affirmation: she experiences an attraction for the positive, creative vision of life shown on the botany slide, for "she had here a glimpse of something working entirely apart from the purpose of the human world" (p. 436). What she glimpsed to her great satisfaction were the completed, "born", unsullied workings of the unconscious that Lawrence describes in *Psychoanalysis and the Unconscious*: "We must discover, if we can, the true unconscious, where our life bubbles up in us, prior to any mentality. The first bubbling life in us, which is innocent of any mental alteration, this is the unconscious. It is pristine, not in any way ideal. It is the spontaneous origin from which it behooves us to live" (p. 13). After Ursula then buoys her own confidence by repeating to herself the complete list of her sunderings, she concludes the listing with a recognition of the powers of the dark, pristine unconscious – that Lawrentian blackness which shortly will swallow the meek Skrebensky on the sand while it also will be the link to Ursula's apprehension of the rainbow:

This inner circle of light in which she lived and moved, wherein the trains rushed and the factories ground out their machine-produce and the plants and the animals worked by the light of science and knowledge, suddenly it seemed like the area under an arc-lamp, wherein the moths and children played in the security of blinding light, not even knowing there was any darkness, because they stayed in the light.   (p. 437)

"Arc-lamp" is the crucial metaphor here, and it translates as an artificial, devitalizing arc – not the natural and procreative arc of birth which becomes the rainbow, but the blinding illumination of a conventionally lighted street lamp.

And with perfect timing for Ursula's developing strength – directly after she receives further evidence in the botany lab that life must not be mind-mechanical, but expressive of the creative unconscious – Anton Skrebensky returns. She previously had waited anxiously for his arrival; yet the anxiety is qualified by her knowledge that they are antagonists who will come together only in a kind of physical truce. Skrebensky arrives with that characteristically pure passion of chauvinism to beg Ursula for the impersonality of some pure sexual passion. Ursula is physically frustrated and she recognizes that her erotic inclinations towards him have in no way diminished. But as Ursula's rhythmic progress has indicated, in the interval since Skrebensky's last departure Ursula has developed a genuine, organic attraction for the "darkness" of unconscious, creative fulfillment. It is the darkness that he uses throughout his writings, the blackness which contains the unseen (and "unknown") depths of potential organic unity that Lawrence demands: "The powerful pristine subjectivity of the unconscious is, on the other hand, the root of all our consciousness and being, darkly tenacious" (*Psychoanalysis and the Unconscious*, p. 28). It is the tenacity of this "root" urge which rhythmically drives Ursula and postpones her exhaustion until the end of the novel. But this "powerful first plane" is easily side-tracked, and Ursula's physical desires get the better of her still maturing judgment; as Lawrence's subtle comment on this error, Ursula mistakenly yields not to the darkness of Skrebensky's soul – that is a bright light! – but to his external seductiveness embodied, quite literally, by the superficial tinge of the traditional "dark" personality of the wayfarer, of the traveler, naturally, to the dark continent of Africa. In essence, Skrebensky trades on his handsome sunburn, and in the beginning he makes quite a bargain for himself. They live in a blinding sexual ecstasy for a few days, but Ursula's expected desire for a deeper, more authentic darkness soon expresses itself with Skrebensky in the destructive way it must for Ursula, the way Lawrence calls "passionate purposive destructive activity" (*Fantasia of the Unconscious*, p. 214). Her relationship to Skrebensky is now described in those familiar terms of battle which recall her former abrasive engagements with him. During their first intimate moments since his return, "she had him" (p. 451), which comes a page after Lawrence's comment that "he had not taken her yet." In effect, he never does. Ursula realizes that "not in any way did he lead into the unknown"

(p. 452). Like Tom and Will, Skrebensky fears that Ursula will leave him; hence his typical desires just for passionate impersonality are superseded by that which he can never have – her unknown soul. Where grandfather Tom Brangwen merely feared the existence of the "unknown" in his wife, pathetically dependent Skrebensky worries that Ursula's dark, unknown quality will motivate her to abandon him. Unlike Will Brangwen, Skrebensky is so desperate that he tries to overlook his dependence on his beloved; he virtually enjoys the opportunity to "sensuously" submit to an inferior position.

But the psychology of the rhythm of Ursula's life continues to assert itself as she becomes restless, and the shaky love affair moves on to Rouen. There Skrebensky's soul is described as "burnt" – as he senses the inevitable rebuffs of Ursula. He is burnt not with the finality of Joan of Arc, but like the baby described in *Psychoanalysis and the Unconscious,* who cried at the severed connection with his mother. His cry is the expression of the silent despairs of Tom and Will, yet the weaker Skrebensky cannot hold it in. His bawling makes Ursula drop her guard in pity and once again establish sexual contact with him. But we recall again Lawrence's apt warning about the female: "God help the man she pities. Ultimately she tears him to pieces". Their sexual communication is very explicit in the use of Lawrence's psychological terminology: "She liked it, the electric fire of the silk under his hands upon her limbs; the fire blew over her, as he drew nearer and nearer to discovery. She vibrated like a jet of electric, firm, *fluid* in response" (p. 477, my italics). All the essentials of perfect communication are present, except the fundamental element of *creativity* that Lawrence stressed in *Psychoanalysis and the Unconscious:* "It is like a lovely, suave, *fluid, creative* electricity that flows in a circuit . . ." (p. 22). A short-circuit is imminent, and it occurs with savage intensity under a brilliant moon, as Ursula's desire to reach the unknown uncovers and crushes his inadequate manhood. This confrontation scene is the cumulative result of Ursula's gradual awareness of Skrebensky's deficiencies, which are summed up in one description of him:

He felt cut off at the knees, a figure made worthless. A horrible sickness gripped him, as if his legs were really cut away, and he could not move, but remained a crippled trunk, dependent, worthless. The ghastly sense of helplessness, as if he were a mere figure that did not exist vitally, made him mad beside himself.

(pp. 461– 462)

Thus the perfect description of the physically and spiritually paralyzed Clifford Chatterley, and Skrebensky is as good as in a wheelchair as he meets Ursula in that climactic scene:

She lay motionless, with wide-open eyes looking at the moon. He came direct to her, without preliminaries. She held him pinned down at the chest, awful. The fight, the struggle for consummation was terrible. It lasted till it was agony to his soul, till he succumbed, till he gave way as if dead, lay with his face buried, partly in her hair, partly in the sand, motionless, as if he would be motionless now for ever, hidden away in the dark, buried, only buried, he only wanted to be buried in the goodly darkness, only that and no more. (p. 479)

He is buried under the moon, annihilated not by a circuit that can be met and returned, but under the "straight line" force of Ursula that heads straight for his soul and is not returned. Lawrence describes the psychology of this rhythm as it *should be* between a couple in *Fantasia of the Unconscious:* "And the night consummation takes place under the spell of the moon. It is one pure motion of meeting and oneing. But even so it is a circuit, not a straight line. . . . And sex union means bringing into connection the dynamic poles of sex in man and woman" (p. 212). Of course this connection is never made in the above scene: Skrebensky lacks the strength to contribute to a circuit, to "one pure motion of meeting and oneing". Or in the specific terminology of rhythm, we know that Lawrence insists that the effective sexual communication reflects a pulsing to-and-fro, a give-and-take rhythm of mutual adjustment and chase that builds to climax. But in this brutal scene, there is no rhythmic exchange – just the one-sided tear of a straight line power that ends with its triumph and the sad sound of "only that and no more". Lawrence defines precisely the rhythmic lacking of this scene in *Fantasia of the Unconscious* once more: "The crisis of their contact in sex connection is the moment of establishment of a new flashing *circuit* throughout the whole sea: the dark, burning red waters of our underworld *rocking in a new dynamic rhythm* in each of us" (p. 203, my italics). As Skrebensky is raped again, there is no circuit, no rocking, and certainly no new dynamic rhythm. It is interesting to note that adolescent Skrebensky is quite similar to Gerald Crich of *Women In Love*. Like Gerald, he is unable to sleep because of thoughts of the beloved to whom he has that emasculating over-sympathetic attachment. And Ursula finds shortly that "there was something distasteful in his coming to her bed" (p. 464), which is the same reaction that Gudrun has in *Women In Love* after her baby-lover steals into her room at night more for mothering than for sex: "There was something monstrous about him, about his juxtaposition against her" (p. 340). But most explicit parallel of all, after Gerald is destroyed by Gudrun, he leaves her like a beaten dog, goes up the cold mountain, and we read:

He was bound to be murdered, he could see it. This was the moment when the death was uplifted, and there was no escape. . . . He had come to the hollow basin of snow, surrounded by sheer slopes and precipices, out of which rose a track that brought one to the top of the mountain. But he wandered unconsciously, till he slipped and fell down, and as he fell something broke in his soul, and immediately he went to sleep. (pp. 465–466)

And because the psychology of the murder is so similar, Skrebensky is described with the identical rhythms of metaphor and syntax:

He felt as if the knife were being pushed into his already dead body. . . . He wandered on a long, long way, till his brain drew dark and he was unconscious with weariness. Then he curled in the deepest darkness he could find, under the seagrass, and lay there without consciousness. (pp. 479–480)

Both Skrebensky and Gerald sense the cause of their murder, they both wander in aimless exhaustion, and they both fall into the sleep of temporary escape. Though Gerald never awakens and Skrebensky "lives" to go to India, the difference in their fate, Lawrence would maintain, is really in degree – not in kind.

E. W. Tedlock, Jr. argues that Ursula's "terrible crisis of health toward the end is caused by the failure with Skrebensky".[12] But Ursula's illness is really the cumulative result of the psychology of rhythm of the novel, of all the exhaustive sunderings she has achieved before the birth of her creative unconscious. Skrebensky has been the last barrier; in no way was her experience a "failure with Skrebensky", but rather a justifiable "separation" from him that necessarily weakens her to the point of pre-birth illness. Ursula is undergoing the predictable pains of her passionate struggle that now take her to the delicate moment of actual birth. While she is sick Lawrence also permits her to conveniently burn out (in fever) the last remnants of Skrebensky, symbolized by her pregnancy, and the removed baby enables a "purified" Ursula to comprehend the appearance of the rainbow. It is a brilliantly consistent metaphorical conclusion: the birth that Ursula strives for is the birth of herself, a birth measured by the success with which she sunders herself from those forces that hold her development back. Her final victory, therefore, is in the celebratory symbolic terms of the abortion of a counterfeit birth. That is, the last barrier to Ursula's birth is torn from within *her* in order for the real Ursula to be born: "Was she with child. . . . What she felt in her heart and her womb she did not know" (p. 483). Yes, very much with child, but for it to be born she must first sunder herself from the embryo inside her that deserves to die.

Middleton Murry, not really a friend of Lawrence's, calls the history of Ursula's striving toward her final vision one of an "annihilation of personality".[13] But this is wrong. In Lawrence's psychology, as dramatized in the rhythm of *The Rainbow*, and enunciated in the essays, what is "false" in Ursula must antedate the birth of her "personality"; for the true, the uncluttered and creative personality of Ursula never manifests itself until her birth at the end of the novel. In short, it is this manifestation of creative being that *is* her birth. Ursula has been un-

[12] E. W. Tedlock, Jr., *D. H. Lawrence, Artist and Rebel* (Albuquerque, 1963), p. 5.
[13] Murry, p. 89.

dergoing the rhythm of the struggle for this birth for nearly three hundred pages, and she has inherited the struggle (not the rhythm) from two generations before her. She has had no true "personality", but was herself both the embryo that is torn from the parent and other forces (as in *Psychoanalysis and the Unconscious),* and the extended embryonic promise of the birth of personality to come. She has safely maneuvered herself through experiences which in the opinion of Lawrence both have adequately tested her ability to withstand the devitalizing tendencies of modern life, and brought to the surface of her "soul" her inclinations toward the desired birth.

Ursula's vision of the horses – whether the animals are real *or* imaginary – I consider both as a symbolic summary of her history of sunderings, and more specifically, a symbolic reflection of her affair with Skrebensky. The horses' fierce flanks ride upon her, and with desperate final effort she manages to avoid them. But as she falls, and runs, and even tries to climb the tree, is she not recalling to us her escape from – indeed, her *purging* of a threat like Skrebensky? Certainly Skrebensky is on her mind at this point. Alan Friedman shows quite persuasively in *The Turn of the Novel* how her letter to Skrebensky proposing marriage and her decision that she had judged him and life incorrectly represents a complete reversal of the pattern (i.e., rhythm) of her belabored struggle toward birth. In her letter she berates herself for her selfish behavior, speaks in the most banal terms of her love for him, and renounces the lessons she has learned in her long independent fight to get this far. Lawrence writes appropriately about this situation in *Psychoanalysis and the Unconscious:* "All this nonsense about love and unselfishness, more crude and repugnant than savage fetishworship. Love is a thing to be *learned,* through centuries of patient effort. It is a difficult complex maintenance of individual integrity . . ." (p. 45). Ursula knows this kind of difficulty and she has demonstrated the patience until the letter to Skrebensky just before the horses appear. But the horses have a mythic, cosmic power totally lacking in Skrebensky: "She went on drawing near. She was aware of the great flash of hoofs, a bluish, iridescent flash surrounding a hollow of darkness. Large,

large seemed the bluish, incandescent flash of the hoof-iron, large as a halo of lightning round the knotted darkness of the flanks" (p. 487). Thus any explanation of this scene, like the moon scenes, must cope with the duality of tone that blends the vague and mythic with the immediate and realistic. Firstly, there are striking similarities between the horses and Skrebensky. The horses are persistent and sensuous, as Lawrence writes:

> She knew the heaviness on her heart. It was the *weight* of the horses. But she would circumvent them. She would bear the *weight* steadily, and so *escape*. She would go straight on, and on, and be gone by. Suddenly the *weight* deepened and her heart grew tense to bear it. Her breathing was labored. But this *weight* also she could bear.... But she went on over the log bridge that their hoofs had churned and drummed, she went on, *knowing* things about them (p. 487, my italics).... She saw the fierce flanks crinkled and as yet *inadequate* (p. 488, my italics).... They were almost *pathetic* now. (p. 489, my italics)

Their oppressive weight, her need to escape them, her knowledge about them, and their ultimate pathos – all themes that relate directly to her experience with Skrebensky. We recall Lawrence on Skrebensky:

> She *knew* him all round, not on any side did he lead into the unknown (p. 473, my italics).... He came to her, and cleaved to her very close, like steel cleaving and clinching on to her.... And Skrebensky was there, an incubus upon her (p. 47).... There was about him some of a horseman's sureness and habitual definiteness of decision, also some of the horseman's *animal* darkness.... She could only feel the dark, *heavy* fixity of his *animal* desire (p. 443, my italics).... Skrebensky, like a load-stone *weighed* on her, the weight of his presence detained her. She felt the burden of him, the blind, persistent, inert burden. He was inert and *weighed* upon her. She sighed in pain (p. 317, my italics).... She thought she had *escaped* [from him]. (p. 453, my italics)

Note that just a paragraph before the appearance of the horses Ursula had made that anti-birth decision to go with Skrebensky and "beat her way back through all the fluctuation, back to stability and security" (p. 486). Out of nowhere the horses *then* appear, almost as the punishing result of this backsliding de-

cision. The rhythm of their attrack, naturally enough, is a coda
to the rhythm of "near-near" that has followed the Brangwen
family through every major crisis in the novel. The description
provides the final example of that pulsing to-and-from movement leading to climax that is at the heart of Lawrence's theory
of repetition:

Some horses were looming in the rain, not near yet. But they were
going to be near. . . . What was it that was drawing near her . . . what
weight oppressing her heart? . . . she went on, drawing near. . . . She
must draw near. . . . She knew she dare not draw near. . . . It was the
crisis. (pp. 486–488)

Thus the fact that the horses are mythically awesome as well as
madly desirous like Skrebensky does not present any overwhelming interpretive problem. When Ursula crushes Skrebensky
under the moon, she crushes him both as a consequence of the
"mythic" heritage (i.e., the moon goddess), and because of her
organic need to express, no matter how destructively, the penetrating powers of her creative unconscious. Similarly, when Ursula avoids the horses, she both symbolically breaks from her
mythic dimension to blossom in the immediate, real present
with a purified unconscious, and interpreted on the non-mythic
level, which includes her experiences with Skrebensky, she refuses to be crushed down by the ponderous weight of animal
desire. Also, in the event that the horses are a vision or dream,
Lawrence puts it all in perfect perspective in *Fantasia of the
Unconscious:* "Most dreams are purely insignificant, and it is
the sign of a weak and paltry nature to pay any attention to them
whatever. Only occasionally they matter. And this is only when
something *threatens* us from the outer mechanical, or acci-
dental *death*-world. When anything threatens us from the world
of death, then a dream may become so vivid that it arouses the
actual soul. And when a dream is so intense that it arouses the
soul – then we must attend to it" (p. 194). After her decision
about joining Skrebensky, Ursula is threatened by a life with
this dull representative of mechanical will and deathly shallow-
ness. Ursula reads the message of the vivid dream, and attends
to it with the psychosomatic killing of a counterfeit embryo and

the organic birth of a real one. Lawrence describes a similar dream of horses in *Fantasia of the Unconscious:* "A man has a persistent passionate fear-dream about horses. He suddenly finds himself among great, physical horses, which may suddenly grow wild. Their great bodies surge madly round him, they rear above him, threatening to destroy him. At any minute he may be trampled down" (p. 199). Although in this passage it is a male that has the vision, the psychological principle which Lawrence feels governs this experience works also in regard to Ursula. Lawrence says that the fact that the horse is presented as an object of terror reflects the dreamer's belief that "the great sensual male activity is the greatest menace". In the long history of Ursula's sundering, it is precisely the sensual activity of the male (cf., the father and Skrebensky) which provides the greatest barriers to her birth. She must wait for Rupert Birkin in *Women In Love* for the man who uses his sexual desire not to obtain power or mollify his insecure ego, but to help establish the perfectly balanced sympathetic and separatist stance.[14]

Ursula will not be "mythic" for the remainder of *The Rainbow* or at all in *Women In Love*. After her escape from the horses, she lies in exhausted solitude against a tree. Her health is gone, but she appears safe and self-secure in her macabre final isolation. Ursula needs only the vision of the rainbow to be "born", and as she rests against the tree she is very much like the person described in *Psychoanalysis and the Unconscious:* "The ample, mature, unfolded individual stands perfect, perfect in himself, but also perfect in harmonious relation to those nearest him and to all the universe" (p. 26). And while Ursula catches her breath after her escape:

As she sat there, spent time and the flux of change passed away from her, she lay as if unconscious upon the bed of the stream, like a stone, unconscious, unchanging, unchangeable, whilst everything rolled by in transience, leaving her there, a stone at rest on the bed of the stream, inalterable and passive, sunk to the bottom of all

[14] Lawrence outlines the intricacies of this stance in his complex discussion of "polarity" in *Psychoanalysis and the Unconscious* and *Fantasia of the Unconscious.*

change. She lay still a long time, with her back against the thorn tree trunk, in her final isolation.   (p. 489)[15]

Note the terms "unconscious" and "final isolation", both indicators of that lonely pause before the well-earned birth of the creative unconscious. Lawrence must have been thinking of this scene of Ursula's exhausted, mind-suspending calm isolation as he writes in *Fantasia of the Unconscious*: "When at last, in all my storms, my whole self speaks, then there is a pause. The soul collects itself into pure silence and isolation – perhaps after much pain. The mind suspends its knowledge and waits. The psyche becomes strangely still. And then, after the pause, there is fresh beginning, a new life adjustment" (p. 165). After much pain the new life adjustment now begins.

Very much alone against the tree, Ursula is in the last process of giving birth to herself, the birth that will be affirmed by her vision of the rainbow. The birth begins with a provocatively worded comment about Ursula's contemplation of Skrebensky's child – phrased in such a way as to lend credence to the idea that Skrebensky's baby relates to a larger symbol, and is an instrument for a more meaningful birth: "Could she not have a child of herself. . . . Was not the child her own affair? all her own affair?" (p. 491). "A child of herself" – and the birth of Ursula Brangwen continues with an orchestra of symbols of procreation, in both explicitly clinical and heavily metaphorical terms. I quote this critical moment at length:

She fought and fought all through her illness to be free of him and his world, to put it aside, to put it aside, into its place. Yet ever anew it gained ascendancy over her, it laid new hold on her. Oh, the unutterable weariness of her flesh, which she could not cast off, nor yet extricate. If she could but extricate herself, if she could but disengage herself from feeling, from her body, from all the vast encumbrances of the world that was in contact with her, from her father, and her mother, and her lover, and all her acquaintance. . . .
    And again, to her feverish brain, came the vivid reality of acorns in February lying on the floor of a wood with their shells burst and

<hr />

15   Lawrence's use of "stone", "stream", and "unchanging", recalls Yeats' use of these terms in "Easter 1916". Lawrence, however, does not feel the ambivalence that Yeats does about this final condition.

discarded and the kernel thrusting forth the clear, powerful shoot, and the world was a bygone winter, discarded, her mother and father and Anton, and college and all her friends, all cast off like a year that has gone by, whilst the kernel was free and naked and striving to take new root, to create a new knowledge of Eternity in the flux of Time. And the kernel was the only reality; the rest was cast off into oblivion.

This grew and grew upon her. When she opened her eyes in the afternoon and saw the window of her room and the faint, smoky landscape beyond, this was all husk and shell lying by, all husk and shell, she could see nothing else, *she was enclosed still, but loosely enclosed. There was a space between her and the shell. It was burst there was a rift in it.* Soon she would have her root fixed in a new Day, her nakedness would take itself the bed of a new sky and a new air, this old, decaying, fibrous husk would be gone.

Gradually she began really to sleep. She slept in the confidence of her new reality. She slept breathing with her soul the new air of a new world. The peace was very deep and enrichening. *She had her root in new ground, she was gradually absorbed into growth.*

(pp. 491–492, my italics)

"Cast off", "extricate", "disengage", "kernel issued naked", "thrust forth", "free and naked", "her root in new ground" – the roll call of birth terms as the novel ends justified by the length of the struggle to be born, and the high priority Lawrence places on the birth itself. In terms of sundering, of the metaphorical break with the womb, Ursula has been born, and she is "perfect" and "mature" in the manner of "the ample . . . individual" Lawrence described in *Psychoanalysis and the Unconscious.* Yet the passionate struggle toward conscious being in the fiction must be consummated by the rainbow symbol at the end. Marvin Mudrick claims that *"The Rainbow* is finally, not about consummation, but about promise."[16] Yet the immense promise or potential of creative birth by Ursula is revealed after her escape from the horses, as she lies against the tree in anti-climactic safety: at this moment she is *free* of all barriers to the complete expression of her creative unconscious, and it remains for her to use the *potential* of such freedom as the means to comprehend the consummating image of the rainbow; it is the com-

---

[16]   Mudrick, p. 45.

prehension that follows the potential which I derived for her in terms of Lawrence's basic psychological principles. For Ursula to use her birth and see and understand the rainbow, Lawrence demands she attain the most sweeping optimistic recognition from that abstract, vague, expanding symbol:

She saw in the rainbow the earth's new architecture, the old, brittle corruption of houses and factories swept away, the world built up in a living fabric of truth, fitting to the overarching heaven.   (p. 495)

But birth or no birth, what do we make of such generalized optimism? Lawrence is pleased about Ursula's achievement, but how can he jump from such pleasure to claims about colliers, houses, truth, etc.? It is here that Mudrick's talk about "promise" is helpful. There is no way to understand Lawrence's sanguine explosion except the simplest: Lawrence considers Ursula's birth and her vision of the rainbow as a kind of "reflective symbol". That is, her emergence into organic being after an extended struggle ending in consummation reflects the ability that certain people have to rise completely above the dead end of mechanical life: "As she grew better, she sat to watch a new creation" (p. 493). Like the conclusion to Zola's novel about colliers, *Germinal*, *germination* is the key – the passing *by example* of the seed of birth from one person to the other:

As she grew better, she sat to watch a new creation. As she sat at her window, she saw the people go by in the street below, colliers, women, children, walking each in the husk of an old fruition, but visible through the husk, the swelling and the heaving contour of the new germination. In the still, silenced forms of the colliers she saw a sort of suspense, a waiting in pain for the new liberation; she saw the same in the false hard confidence of the women. The confidence of the women was brittle. It would break quickly to reveal the strength and patient effort of the new germination.

Thus the optimism of "over-arching heaven" – the symbolic conclusion to all the arch imagery of the Brangwen generations – reflects Lawrence's belief, however naive, that the history of the birth Ursula achieves is not an impossible pattern of psychological development; it is an archetype for transformation, an extended example of one person's ability to stick to the rhythm of necessary sundering to the very end.[17] This archetype represents the potential that most people have to achieve some degree of organic freedom.[18] In a letter about *The Rainbow*, Lawrence repeats his call for the germination of the Word, and he also conveniently recapitulates the two central dangers to birth that he dramatized throughout the novel: an emasculated man's over-sympathetic attachment to his woman, and the woman's marriage to blood-intimacy. It is a summary of the rhythm of the novel:

You ask me about the message of *The Rainbow*. I don't know myself what it is: except the older world is done for, toppling on top of us; and that it's no use the men looking to the women for salvation, nor the women looking to sensuous satisfaction for their fulfillment. There must be a new world.[19]

Ursula Brangwen's birth follows her inherited passionate struggle into conscious being, her personal battle that saw the sundering destruction of the forces that denied her right to be born. "There must be a new world" Lawrence says, and although this necessity may be arguable to some, and the achievement of it in Lawrence's terms impossible to others, the scrupulous care with which he charts the psychology of the rhythm to achieve it illustrates his integration of the aesthetic with the prophetic.

---

[17] Elizabeth Drew relates this Jungian concept of an archetype for transformation to T. S. Eliot in *T. S. Eliot: The Design Of His Poetry* (New York, 1949). My term "reflective symbol", incidentally, works for the end of Eliot's "The Wasteland". See also Rieff, *The Triumph of the Therapeutic,* for relevant discussion of archetypes.
[18] Obviously, people like Rico in *St. Mawr,* Clifford Chatterley, Gerald Crich and Skrebensky are innately dead and their "achievement" is severely limited.
[19] *Letters,* p. 422.

SELECTED BIBLIOGRAPHY

Abbott, C. C., ed., *The Letters of Gerald Manley Hopkins to Robert Bridges* (London, 1955).

Brown, E. K., *Rhythm In The Novel* (Toronto, 1950).

Drew, Elizabeth, *T. S. Eliot: The Design Of His Poetry* (New York, 1949).

Ford, George, *Double Measure* (New York, 1965).

Forster, E. M., *Aspects of the Novel* (New York, 1958).

Friedman, Alan, *The Turn of the Novel* (New York, 1966).

Goodheart, Eugene, *The Utopian Vision of D. H. Lawrence* (Chicago, 1963).

Lawrence, D. H., *Aaron's Rod* (New York, 1961).

—, *Fantasia of the Unconscious* (New York, 1960).

—, *Lady Chatterley's Lover* (New York, 1962).

—, *The Man Who Died* (New York, 1959).

—, *Phoenix: The Posthumous Papers of D. H. Lawrence* (New York, 1936).

—, *Psychoanalysis and the Unconscious* (New York, 1960).

—, *The Rainbow* (New York, 1961).

—, *St. Mawr* (New York, 1959).

—, *Sex, Literature, and Censorship* (New York, 1959).

—, *Studies in Classic American Literature* (New York, 1964).

—, *Women In Love* (New York, 1960).

Leavis, F. R., *D. H. Lawrence: Novelist* (London, 1955).

Moore, Harry T., ed., *The Collected Letters of D. H. Lawrence* (New York, 1962).

—, *The Intelligent Heart* (New York, 1962).

Moynahan, Julian, *The Deed of Life* (Princeton, 1963).

Mudrick, Marvin, "The Originality of The Rainbow," in *Spectrum,* III (Winter, 1959).

Murray, J. Middleton, *D. H. Lawrence: Son of Woman* (London, 1954).

Rieff, Philip, *The Triumph of the Therapeutic* (New York, 1966).

Spilka, Mark, ed., *D. H. Lawrence: A Collection of Critical Essays* (Englewood Cliffs, N.J., 1963).

—, *The Love Ethic of D. H. Lawrence* (Bloomington, Indiana, 1953).

Tedlock, E. W., Jr., *D. H. Lawrence, Artist and Rebel* (Albuquerque, N. M., 1963).

Tindall, William York, ed., *The Later D. H. Lawrence* (New York, 1952).

Tiverton, Father William, *D. H. Lawrence and Human Existence* (New

York, 1951).

Van Ghent, Dorothy, *The English Novel: Form and Function* (New York, 1961).

Vivas, Eliseo, *D. H. Lawrence: The Failure and the Triumph of Art* (Evanston, Illinois, 1960).

de proprietatibus litterarum

Series Practica

Dfl.

de proprietatibus litterarum

Dfl.